LYNN'S STORY

LYNN KAMPFER

DEDICATION

This story of my faith journey and coming into relationship with God is dedicated to my children, Cory and Kinsey. You are the greatest gifts I have been given and have brought me more joy than I could have ever imagined. Thank you for your ongoing love and support during very trying times. You were always my inspiration to keep moving forward and to never give up. I love you more than words can express.

CONTENTS

LYNN'S STORY

1

THE CRISIS

God, where are You? It's cold. It's bleak. It's Sunday at 6:30 a.m. on a January morning and I'm just sitting here in my car. Am I crazy? I've never felt so despondent. And what has happened to my life? A few years ago I was soaring and couldn't understand why I was so blessed; now my life has gone to hell. I hate it! And I am so ashamed. How did I get here? How did I sink so low so quickly? My God, it's cold in this car.

My mood matches the dark morning. The sleet blurs my vision as I look out the windshield. Maybe this is good because no one can see me. If they did, they'd think I was nuts. Maybe I am nuts. Who sits in her car in the driveway at 6:30 on a Sunday morning in January?

I am losing it; and I am so, so tired. I can't endure another sleepless and tormented night trying to figure out how I got where I am. It's not that I want to do this, but when I get into bed and stop moving, my mind begins to race and replays everything that's happened in the past several years. I desperately need sleep, and I know I'm not thinking clearly.

I used to pride myself on being strong; I was always able to figure stuff out, or at least mask the problem until I came up with a solution. Now I'm not sure I can even drive across town without crashing into something,

"Lynn, get a grip and figure out a plan – your kids need you – you can't give up."

Although I would never commit suicide, at this moment, I understand why people do. Some days it just hurts to live and this is going to another rough day. My mind is working in slow motion, but I'm getting some ideas: OK, I can drive to the local hospital, walk into the ER and say, "I need to be committed."

I'm not sure if you need a referral or if you have to fail some kind of a mental test to get them to admit you, but I'm sure I can easily fail any test in my current state. I really don't want anyone to talk to me – I just want to get into that hospital bed, pull the covers up over my head, and never come out. But then they would send in psychologists to evaluate me and I am not up to talking to anyone, let alone a psychologist. Furthermore, at work I am always the one who counsels people. I'm not sure I want to be on the other side of the chair.

No, this will never work, because I don't want any interaction and I'll lose control in the hospital. Oh Lord, it would be embarrassing if people found out I was there. I also need to get back to work to earn money to support the family.

OK, keep thinking: I could go to church, but I look pathetic. I haven't had a shower, I'm in my old jeans, and tears have ruined any remaining makeup from the previous day. Maybe I'll just go back in the house but something tells me this isn't a good idea. Sundays used to be very special: they were "family days" and my husband, our two kids and I would spend the day together, and then eat dinner in front of the TV (something that was never done during the week).

I loved Sundays but now they are endless and lonely. I so want to be alone but then when I'm alone, I don't know what to do with myself. Why can't I go back to my blessed life? Will I ever be really happy again?

An hour has passed and I need to figure out what to do. Why can't the sun ever shine in Toledo? I so hate these bleak, winter days. Alright, I can do this. I'm going to go to church and sit in a corner where no one will see me, hope for a good message, and then bolt out of the door once the service ends. I need to concentrate as I pull out of the driveway; by now the roads are getting slick and I feel like I'm in a daze. I can do this – I have to do this – my kids need me.

I pull into the parking lot at church and thank goodness there are very few cars. I slink in the door and find a nice quiet place in the corner. I am the only one in the church and the lights are dim. I find a seat and sit, exhausted. At least I'm warm. I should have a good hour before I have to fake a smile and say hi to anyone. Tears start streaming down my face. I've never felt so alone in my life.

Tell me this isn't happening! A man is walking towards me, coming down my row of seats. I can't believe it but he is now sitting right next to me. What is he thinking? There are nearly 1,000 seats in the church and he has to sit right next to me? I don't even know him. He is a very big African-American man with dreadlocks.

Hey, this may be church, but I'm just going to tell him to find another seat, as I desperately need to be alone with my thoughts and tears. Just as I'm about ready to tell him to move, he reaches down and takes my hand and just holds it – he doesn't say a word. His hand is strong, yet gentle; his fingers curl around my hand and totally cover it. What is going on? One minute I want to scream at him for sitting right by me and the next minute I feel strangely comforted by him.

This is not my "norm" to be holding hands in church with a man I have never laid eyes on. But I'm keenly aware that at this moment, I have a sensation of peace – deep, pure peace. And it is so good. I have not felt peace for so long. He kindly whispers in my ear,

"It looks like you're going through a storm." There is no need to respond; he can see my pain.

The man holds my hand until the service starts. Tears are still streaming down my face but I feel safe for the moment and miles away from sitting in that cold car thinking about going to the psych unit. At the end of the service, he hands me a piece of paper with a radio station's call numbers on it. He quietly says,

"Listen to this station at 8 a.m. tomorrow," and then he is gone.

I wonder if this is a sign from God. I so want to believe that You are real. I so want to believe that You are always with me, but this is really hard. Okay, for today I have hope. I feel like You are with me (at least right now). I'll have to think more about this later but now I know I will make it through this long, cold Sunday.

I manage to get a decent night's sleep, but Monday morning comes with a vengeance. I don't like spending Sundays alone, but I'm wondering how I will ever manage to get through all the interactions and demands of the week. I drag myself out of bed and head off to work. As I get closer to the office, the tears start coming down. Darn it! I look terrible now, a daily occurrence it seems. I had made a pact with myself to not walk into the office until I could muster up a smile. I drive over to a little cemetery and park.

Although the day is still cold and bleak, it's peaceful and quiet. I beg God to help me get through this day and I remind Him that He promises that He will always be with me. The peace I had yesterday is now a distant memory. I've got to get to work – I can't lose my job right now.

I leave the cemetery and allow myself to drive around the block three times so I can pull myself together before going in. God – You've got to stop these tears – I need you right now! I look at the clock – it's 8 a.m. and I need to be in the office. All of the sudden I remember the man with the dreadlocks who gave me the radio station to listen to at 8 a.m. Shoot – what did I do with that sheet of paper? I'm rummaging through all my notebooks trying to find it.

Finally, I find the crumpled up piece of paper and quickly tune in the radio station. Just as I find it, I hear the announcer say,

"We have a caller."

I'm not really in the mood to listen to people call in and chat, but I stay tuned in. The caller starts to talk and it is the man from church. He says,

"I met a woman named Lynn yesterday who is going through a storm and I went home and wrote a poem for her."

He then reads the most beautiful and encouraging poem – one he had written just for me! The poem touches me in a way I cannot explain. Now the tears are really pouring down my cheeks, but they are tears of gratitude. Was this You God? Did You really orchestrate all of this? Did You hear my little prayer at the cemetery and answer it in such a profound and touching way? I know people tell me You are real and watch over us. I need to know this for myself! How was I to know that my husband of 30 years is a felon? I'm scared and need You more than You know. But, maybe (just maybe) You do know?

2

EARLY YEARS

When I was growing up, God was just there, as good addition to my very nice life. Though I had no relationship with God, to speak of, my parents made sure our family went to church every Sunday. It didn't mean much; however, I couldn't wait to get out and go home to eat my mom's homemade pecan rolls (a Sunday treat)!

When I got to junior high, I was expected to attend two years of weekly confirmation classes. I did this, got confirmed and was able to take communion at the regular church service. The most memorable part of my confirmation was that I got to wear my first pair of heels, so you know where my priorities were. I felt very grown-up as I stood in front of the church. My grandmother gave me a Bible in the fifth grade, and though I never looked much at it, I did love the picture on the cover of Jesus with all the little children gathered around. He looked so loving and kind. I don't remember praying much, except for the few times I thought a robber was in the house or at holiday dinners.

To me, being godly meant being nice to people, helping those in need, following the rules, and staying out of trouble. If I had a relationship with God, it was superficial. But, I was always very aware of how blessed I was. I knew our family had more than most. Sometimes I felt guilty about this, but most of the time, I was just genuinely appreciative of all we had been given.

I was the youngest of three children. My sister was two years older and we were very close. She looked out for me and I learned much about the "next stages" in life by watching and listening to her. Even when we had our own bedrooms, we often chose to sleep together. I loved having a big sister!

My brother was six years older and this large age difference didn't allow for the same closeness I had with my sister. We got along fine but didn't have many common interests.

Although my parents didn't talk much about God, they did good things that helped people. For example, when I was in the second grade they took in a young girl who was having problems at home. My dad managed a department store and she had stolen a dress. Well, the store policy was to prosecute all shoplifters, so she was taken to court.

In the course of the legal proceedings, however, my parents realized this girl's parents were unable to care for her, so they brought her home to live with us. I didn't think much of it at the time but now can appreciate just how challenging this must have been for my parents and family. And indeed, there were some rocky times. But there were many more good times.

My foster sister remained with us through college until she got married and moved out of state. We all remained in close contact until she died in 2009.

My childhood was safe, secure and very happy. My parents had traditional roles. My dad went to work every day and my mom stayed home with the three kids. They were a perfect complement for each other. Though my dad was a man of few words, he lived his values. We watched him work hard, be financially responsible, demonstrate discipline and show us, by his actions, the importance of character.

My mom was very outgoing, highly educated and lots of fun. She taught us to love books, to be inquisitive about life and to be open to new things. She also conveyed social graces. My parents had lived through the Depression so, as you can imagine, nothing was ever wasted at our house. I don't remember a lot of drama growing up. I had the usual fights with my siblings and the neighborhood kids but nothing out of the norm. I felt loved, valued and safe.

My school was just a few blocks from our house and at noon every day, the doors opened to let everyone go home for lunch. My mom was always there to greet us with something good to eat. On special occasions she would drive to school and surprise us by taking us to McDonald's. Oh, how I loved those days!

The teachers at our school were excellent and had high expectations. Virtually everyone went on to gain a college degree. So, it was a shock to my parents when my first grade teacher told them I didn't have the aptitude to go to college and that I would be lucky if I graduated from high school. She recommended that my parents find a trade where I could make a living. Thank goodness they didn't believe this and never mentioned it to me until I was much older and had graduated from college.

Every house in our neighborhood was filled with kids. We spent most evenings after completing our homework, of course, playing kick the can, rain on the roof, hide and seek, tag and other games. We were allowed to stay outside until the street lights came on. I called most of the moms and dads in the neighborhood "aunt" and "uncle" and felt very much at home with their families. Sleepovers and eating meals with the neighbors were common. All the moms watched out for the kids, and the kids knew and trusted the parents.

One of my bigger crises was when I was in first grade and my mom told me that I could no longer play football with the boys. I loved sports, so I was devastated. She told me the neighbors were concerned that I was acting too much like a boy and needed to be more like a young lady. I was crushed! Playing dolls was boring compared to the fun and challenge of football!

Not taking part in a team sport was an ongoing issue for me because there were no sports for girls at our school, not unusual at that time in our nation's history. I was always envious of the boys who participated in so many cool things while we had to watch them in the stands, or make the few available spots on the cheerleading squad.

When I was eight years old, I met a friend who swam on a community swim team and I begged my parents to let me join. After some thought, they finally agreed to this. I was elated and this began a lifetime love of swimming. Our family spent summers at a cottage we shared with another family. The moms and kids drove there the day after school got out and returned on Labor Day. Summers were awesome! When our morning chores were completed, we spent the entire rest of the day on the water. We had a canoe, small speed boat, sailboat, pontoon raft and a big speed boat.

After a morning of waterskiing, we would often have ten kids (ages 6-12) on the pontoon raft we motored around. When we anchored, all the kids jumped off the raft and pontoons into the water. It wasn't unusual to be jumped upon or hit by the pontoons as one of the "big kids" dove into the water, which jerked the raft to one side.

Looking back, it seems we must have had angels watching over us, as there were very few accidents. We spent evenings playing different card games; there was no TV. It was always fun when the dads arrived for the weekend. We would run to greet them and share all we had done during the week. They were as happy to see us as we were to see them.

The dads spent most of the weekend doing odd jobs, which always seemed strange to me because I wanted them to relax and spend the day on the water with us. They seemed to love to work together, though, and also to have fun. Occasionally they would start a water balloon fight, which would spread to all the families in the neighboring cottages. These water fights could last up to two days and were crazy and exciting.

One of my best memories is those Sunday mornings my dad and I rose early to get donuts and penny candy. He would row the boat while I swam to the store at the end of the lake. We took the donuts back to the cottage, but the penny candy was just for us. We made sure to eat all of it before we got back to the cottage because candy before breakfast was not allowed. These Sunday boat trips are some of my best memories with my dad.

Swimming was becoming a really important part of my life. When I was ten years old, I heard about a swimming camp in Canada run by Matt Mann who coached the men's Olympic team as well as the men's team at the University of Michigan. I asked my parents if we could drive to Ann Arbor, Michigan, to find out more about the camp. They agreed. I loved what I heard and wanted to go. The camp lasted seven weeks and cost $500, which was a huge amount of money at the time. I was really nervous when I asked my parents if I could go, and I was even more shocked when they said, "Yes."

This camp had a profound impact on my life. Its motto was, "We don't sew beads on belts," which emphasized that there were no arts and crafts, except to paint your canoe paddle.

It was on a beautiful lake in northern Ontario. A typical day consisted of a swim workout at 7 a.m. breakfast, two hours of individual sports, dry land exercises, a second swim workout, lunch, rest hour, two hours of team sports, a third swim workout, dinner, and then an additional activity or a fourth swim workout. If anyone ever said, "I can't" they would immediately be told to run the cross county course, even if it was dark. "I'll try" was acceptable, but never, "I can't."

The camp directors were always coming up with ideas to physically challenge us. One summer when I was twelve they decided the campers would all take a 50-mile hike (part of the President's physical fitness challenge). The day before the walk, I couldn't find my tennis shoes and was asking lots of campers if anyone had an extra pair. One girl reluctantly gave me her brand new saddle shoes, which were stiff and too small for my feet. I wore them but after five miles had so many blisters that I could hardly walk. I ended up walking the next 45 miles in my socks.

We also lifted weights at camp, something that I was not allowed to do at home. My mom was concerned that I would get big muscles and start to look like a boy. I wasn't worried since I never saw any girl at camp who looked remotely like a guy.

I loved this camp and ended up going for seven summers. It was so liberating. I hated the thought of going back to school where I was only allowed to play half-court basketball and have three dribbles before passing the ball (any more than this was thought to be way too strenuous for a girl). I had trouble expressing to my parents how much camp meant to me. I think I always felt badly that it cost them so much money.

Many years later I wrote them a long letter telling them the positive impact the camp had had on my life. They were genuinely surprised and very pleased.

BILL ENTERS THE SCENE

I started dating Bill, my future husband, my junior year in high school. I had known him since Kindergarten and had my first "date" with him in first grade when he invited me to his house to go sledding and have hot chocolate. Bill was fun, attentive, and always had something interesting to do or see. He had a broad range of interests and we enjoyed formal dances as well as quiet walks in the park. Life was comfortable and safe with Bill. We could talk about anything and I felt I could always count on him.

I did graduate from high school in spite of the dire prediction of my first grade teacher. Not only that but I was accepted at the University of Michigan! I loved college and my newfound freedom. I majored in education and joined the women's swim team. I pledged a sorority, which was probably more important to my mom than to me. Life was new and exciting.

I continued to date Bill, though he was at Ohio State, as well as other young men at college. After my sophomore year, I decided to transfer schools. Bill and I were getting more serious and I felt it was important to see him every day before making a commitment.

Being with Bill at Ohio State was great. We had a fun group of friends and studied hard and played even harder. This was also during the Vietnam War when there was much unrest.

When the school closed after the shootings at Kent State University I went home, realizing how fortunate I was to be at school. I couldn't wait to get back after the two-week cool down period. I was determined to experience as much as possible while I was at school. I was well aware that this was a very special time in my life. Bill proposed to me the semester before I graduated from Ohio State. This was the normal course of things at that time:

graduate from college and get married a few weeks later. He gave me a pair of golf shoes, one of which contained a diamond ring.

My mom planned the wedding while I finished school, and I was married eight weeks after graduation. Bill and I both wanted to experience new things, and we were thrilled when he got a job in Los Angeles. We drove to LA right after the wedding, and I felt so grown up. We were going to have a wonderful adventure in California, and I was certain we would never return to Ohio.

I worked at the Beverly Hills YMCA and was a traveling swim instructor on the side. It was great! I went from backyard pool to backyard pool and taught kids to swim. Bill was a golf professional at a country club. These jobs gave us enough money to experience California. We spent much time at the ocean, mountains and desert and we traveled around the southwest. Life was wonderful.

Two years later, Bill was offered a better job at a country club in Atlanta, Georgia, which he accepted. After spending a year in Atlanta, we decided Toledo wasn't such a bad place to live, after all. We wanted to start a family and believed Toledo would be a great place to raise children. We moved back and quickly found jobs, which were easy to get in those days. Bill got into the insurance business, and I found work at the local YWCA.

Things were moving along and then great news! After five years of marriage I was pregnant. We had waited a long time to have kids and were more than ready to begin this new journey. I was a little nervous and wondered if I would be a good mom. After all I had some pretty big shoes to fill from my own mom and I really wanted to do well in my new role.

My pregnancy was easy, and I was able to swim right up until the delivery. Seeing our new little boy, Cory, was amazing and miraculous. It was the highlight of my life. I felt such a bond with him and wanted to love and protect him forever. Cory was a very focused, smart, and responsible little boy. When he made up his mind to do something, nothing could deter him. He was also delightfully funny and able to find the humor in any situation.

Two years later I was pregnant again but ended up losing the baby at eight months. This was devastating, but I gained a new appreciation for the gift of life. I was ecstatic when Kinsey was born two years later. Just like Cory's, her birth was the highlight of my life. How blessed I was to have a little boy and a little girl. Kinsey had her own unique personality, which was quite different from Cory's. She was spontaneous, compassionate and a free spirit. She always had to experience things and wouldn't take anyone's word that "a stove is really hot," or "don't jump in the water if it is over your head." In spite of many accidents and close calls, Kinsey had a wonderfully resilient spirit and always recovered quickly.

Bill and I wanted our children to experience the same great childhood we had, so we bought my parents' house so they could grow up where we grew up. They would walk to the same school and come home for lunch (when Bill or I could be there) just like we did when we were that age. We did many things as a family and sought out friends with kids the same age as ours.

We visited Grandma and Grandpa in Florida every year and took a spring and fall trip to Fire Island (in New York) and a summer trip with the cousins. We also went on lots of camping trips at the national parks out west. The kids were very involved with sports, and Bill and I got to know and enjoy their friends who would often come to dinner or spend the night.

Once again, life was good. It was also mapped out. We planned to buy a condo on a golf course in Florida after the kids graduated from college. We would retire when we were 55 and spend our winters in the condo and summers back in Toledo. I knew we were blessed but also felt somewhat entitled to this wonderful life; we had worked hard and done the "right things" to make this happen.

God was never a big part of our family life. Bill and I didn't take the kids to church because Sunday was the only unscheduled day and we wanted to keep it that way. When Cory was in second grade, we took him to a wedding and the preacher mentioned God. Cory loudly blurted out,

"Who is God"?

Bill and I were embarrassed and a bit chagrined so we decided it would be a good idea to begin attending church. Some friends had asked us to go with them, so without too much thought we joined their church. Although we went to services most Sundays, God remained simply a nice add-on to our very good life. Of course, I would tell everyone that I believed in God, and I did, on some level. I just had no idea that there could be so much more to experience as my relationship with God became stronger.

3

GOD'S LEADING

As I look back on my life, it seems apparent that God was always leading me, even when I didn't know it. It is clear to me now that He wanted to reel me into a relationship with Him. For some reason, though, I was not able to hear His voice, maybe because I was always pretty self-sufficient and thought I was doing a good job or so I thought of running my own life. Plus, God had many bigger issues to deal with than my small problems, or so I thought. In spite of feeling that I didn't really need God, I can see now there were two crucial times He took the wheel and changed my course.

The first was when the children were small. Back then, I was working full-time at a hospital, completing my master's degree, swimming on a master's team and very involved in numerous family activities. In the middle of all this, my back went out and I was confined to bed for three weeks. Lying in bed all day and just reading and thinking was a new experience.

During those long days, I kept hearing,

"Cut down on your hours and reorder your life. You are not living according to your values."

I had always said that my family was my most important value, but my busy life did not reflect it. I was humbled but grateful to hear this message. At the time I would have attributed the voice to me, believing I had a rare opportunity to think through my life and change courses. Now, however, I see this event as the first time I was aware of God taking the wheel from me.

I would cut down on my hours, and I had plenty of time to think through a plan. I was almost finished with my master's degree. All I had to do was ask my manager at the hospital if I could go part-time to spend more time with my family. I felt certain this request would be granted as part-timers saved the company money. So, I was surprised when my manager said, "No," without leaving any room for further discussion.

Now I had to come up with a new plan. Even though I was getting my master's degree in education, I didn't want to teach in a school system. One area that had always interested me was training.

At the time, I was coordinating conferences for the hospital. My manager was in charge of several functions, including training. I had asked her several times how I could get into training and was told each time that I did not have the required skill set and probably never would. At the time, I thought it was good she said, "No" because I secretly lacked the confidence that I could succeed in training.

Though I had always been able to easily speak in front of people, something happened between my junior and senior year in high school (I have no idea what it was) and I was no longer able to do this. At the start of my senior year, I vividly remember being called on to give an oral report on the book *Emma* and I could barely get any words out. I felt like I was having a panic attack and was humiliated in front of my classmates.

At that point, I made a decision to avoid all public speaking, and I did, for the next ten years. Finally, though, I got sick and tired of being afraid and decided to do something about it. I joined Toastmasters (I was the only woman with twenty-five men) and after three years of weekly meetings, finally overcame my fear of public speaking. I actually found it humorous to think if I did get into training that I would be making my living off my "biggest fear," but I was willing to give it a try. Unfortunately, I quickly realized that this was not going to happen at my current place of employment.

Less than a month after being told I could not go part-time and would never be able to be a trainer, a consultant came to the hospital to deliver a program. I really liked this man and found out that he was in human resources at a company in town. I went up to him after the session and asked,

"Do you need a part-time trainer at your company, because I'm looking to do this and believe we would work really well together."

As it turned out, he did need a part-time trainer and in the next six weeks I left the hospital, completed my master's degree, and was working as a part-time trainer at a new company. Going to this company was one of the best decisions I ever made in my life. Actually, I now believe that God was leading me to a place that not only was value-centered but would turn out to be a refuge during turbulent times.

The second time I believe God spoke to me was when I was at a park. By this time, Bill and I had been married for fourteen years. I had just taken a hike and was sitting on a bench enjoying the beauty of nature before facilitating a training session. A message came to me totally out of the blue,

"You need to go through your husband's files at work."

What was this all about? I totally trusted Bill. Why on earth would I ever go through his files? The command was so strong that it scared me, and I made up my mind to do this as soon as I returned home. As luck would have it, Bill was going out of town the next day (a Saturday) to play golf. No one would be in the office, and this would be the perfect time to go through his files. I didn't even know what I was looking for but started meticulously going through each file.

Within ten minutes, I found something that shocked me: Bill had borrowed $200,000 to loan to a friend. He had never told me about this and we certainly didn't have this kind of money. What in the world was he thinking? I got hold of him on the golf course and told him to come home right away.

When I confronted him with what I had found, he didn't have much of an explanation except to say the money was loaned to a friend to help with a business venture. Bill said he hoped to eventually be a part of this venture. I was furious.

We had planned to take a vacation the next week, but I told him I needed to get away from him (I wasn't sure where I was going to go). I called a friend in Pittsburgh and asked if I could come and stay with her for a while. Bill was an excellent father so I knew the kids would be well cared for when I walked out of the house.

I did a lot of soul-searching that week in Pittsburgh. This was a huge betrayal and had large financial and emotional consequences. We had always had an understanding to be partners in all big decisions. This was certainly a big decision, and I couldn't believe he did this without ever talking to me.

Did I really want to stay with this man? What about the kids? They adored their father and I wasn't even sure I could support them on my part-time salary. I remembered hearing in church that we should forgive people seventy-times-seven. What was that supposed to mean? When is enough, enough?

I did much talking and praying with my friend. After a week I returned home and Bill and I had a long discussion. I decided to forgive him and he swore he would never do anything like that again. But, deep down I'm not sure I totally trusted him where money was concerned.

Bill and I paid off the loan. His friend's business venture never took off and we never received a penny from him. In spite of this hurdle, the next ten years were good ones. The kids were growing up and kept us very busy. I was proud of them and loved watching them go through the different stages of life. They meant everything to me, and I was so happy to be working part-time so I could be there to support them in their many activities.

Bill and I were doing well and extraordinarily happy with each other. I was still working as a trainer at the same company and enjoyed my work and the constant contact I got to have with all the employees. Although I never had any formal training in counseling, many employees confided in me and I was able to help them with their problems. I always considered this a great privilege.

Bill was still in the insurance business and now had his own agency. We had beautiful children, a nice home, great health, plenty of money, terrific friends, and a wonderful family life. Life was not just blessed, but over-blessed. My awareness of how lucky we were prompted me to make an appointment with our pastor. I had never done anything like that before but needed to ask him why God gave so much to certain people and so little to others. It didn't seem fair and if He is a just God, then I would expect Him to bless everyone.

I also asked my pastor to tell me what faith was. He had been preaching on it, but it didn't make much sense to me. We talked about God, but I found I had more questions than answers. He gave me some books to read on faith, and I read them but didn't connect at all. I knew there must be more to learn. I didn't do much praying in those days, but felt this strong urge to ask God to help me understand this elusive word – faith.

Two weeks after I said this prayer, my life fell apart. When I look back from this vantage point, I see it was an opportunity to understand, at a very deep level, what faith is. At the time, however, it felt like my world had come to an end.

4

TROUBLE

For the past five years, Bill had been the executor of a trust for his aunt. She had been living alone about 200 miles from us and was showing signs of dementia. The owners of the apartment where she lived called and said she was acting bizarre and they wanted her out of the building. This was not a surprise to us as we had all seen some of these symptoms.

Bill and his family decided she needed to live in a home where she would be safe and taken care of. We found a good place for her in our city and Bill managed her money. Although it was hard to communicate with her, our family visited her often and got her out as much as possible. We were all good to her, including Bill. She wasn't a hardship to us; she was family.

Then Bill came home one evening and told me his aunt's trust fund was missing one million dollars. Though shocked, I thought there must be some mistake and that we would get to the bottom of it. As far as I knew, Bill had done a great job managing this fund and had certainly spent much time with his aunt. The bank that handled the trust and Bill's parents were going to conduct an investigation to find out what had taken place.

There were many meetings and court hearings, none of which I attended. Within a few months, it was determined that the trust was indeed missing one million dollars. It was also determined that Bill had taken this money. How could this be? I had never forgotten the incident ten years earlier when Bill had borrowed money to loan to his friend. But making a foolish loan was in a far different category from stealing money. Furthermore, we had plenty of money and there had been no other issues since he'd made that mistake.

I was devastated, angry and confused. What could have happened? Bill was shaken and vowed to find out what had taken place. After a few days, he gathered our family together (the kids were now in junior high and high school) and tearfully told us what had happened. He said he had several accounts at the same bank and that "the friend" to whom he loaned the money years before had finally paid him back (plus ten years of interest and penalties).

He said his friend told him that he deposited the money in Bill's account at the bank. He said that account contained both money from his insurance business and from his aunt. Bill said he had spent the money to repay business loans because he thought it was the money owed to him from his friend. With time, Bill said he realized his friend had lied and never did deposit any money.

Bill took full responsibility for this "mistake" and seemed to be devastated. He said he couldn't believe this had happened and vowed to make everything right. The kids were in tears and promised they would do everything they could to help in this situation. I was heartsick and believed he was telling the truth. It was unthinkable that anything else could have happened. We would stick together and make it through all of this, but our lives were about to dramatically change.

Bill's parents were very involved because the aunt was his dad's sister. They told us we had one year to put one million dollars back in the account or they would prosecute Bill and he would go to prison. This was a hard thing to hear from my in-laws. This was not how families were supposed to operate, and relations became very strained. The next year was a blur. All of our accounts were immediately emptied. We had to provide a list to the bank of all of our investments and any property we owned. All investments were cashed in and given to the bank.

Next came our property. The office building, which we owned and rented out to other tenants, was sold. Next was our house and the cottage on Fire Island in New York, given to me by an uncle. How would this be handled? Where would we live, if everything went? My family knew what happened and always stood by us. They couldn't have been more supportive. They worked with the courts and each bought a piece of property so this money could be applied to the deficit.

My sister and her husband bought our house, and my parents bought the cottage on Fire Island. This was humbling. I was incredibly grateful, but embarrassed and humiliated at the same time. I was used to being the giver, not the recipient of help. It was a blessing to be able to stay in our home by paying rent to my sister. We were on a very tight budget. Every available dollar went to repay this money.

Cory and Kinsey were amazing during this time.

They supported their dad in every way, as did I. The thought of Bill in prison was unimaginable. It was a turbulent year, but with the help from my family, we did manage to come up with the million dollars. Bill would not be going to prison and we could now try to rebuild our life. Although we were financially wiped out, we were in good health and our family remained incredibly close.

During this time, I began talking to God more and more. Why did He let this happen? I was slowly getting a better understanding of faith:

The substance of things hoped for, the evidence of things not seen.

I hoped for a lot during this time but didn't see evidence of much of it coming to pass. I had a need to go deeper with God so I asked Him to lead us to a church where I could learn more. A wonderful pastor knew about our situation and offered to give us counseling though we did not attend his church.

After a year, we joined this new church. This was a good move; my eyes were opened and I learned much as I studied the Bible. The road to recovery was beginning to show some promise. A marriage is "for better or worse" and we had just endured some of the worst, but now things were going to change for the better or so I thought.

Things did change, but not in the way we expected. Approximately 18 months later, the IRS caught up with Bill's situation. They determined that Bill had indeed taken one million dollars (even if it was through a terrible mistake) and that this money was never declared as income on his tax returns, which I had also signed. The heat was on and things began to move very quickly. There were many hearings and depositions. I was not a part of most of these and was advised to get my own attorney. We were already struggling financially and all these attorneys took things over the edge.

As always, our family remained solidly behind Bill. On a beautiful day in September, Bill asked me to come with him to yet another hearing at court. I went to the courthouse with him but he told me that I was not allowed to be in the hearing. He was in a room for a few hours and I just walked around the courthouse, which I disliked but was getting used to doing. When Bill walked out of the hearing, he was visibly shaken; his face was ashen, and he said,

"I can't believe what just happened. They are sending me to prison for tax fraud."

When I said, "There must be some mistake."

Bill assured me that there was and that we would fight things. He said he might have to be in prison for a few months but that we would get things turned around in an appeal. Once again, I believed him and stood by him. Calling our children to tell them that their dad - whom they adored - was going to prison was one of the most painful things I have ever endured. Kinsey had just left for her freshman year at Indiana University and Cory was a junior at The University of Georgia. Both kids were in shock and came home immediately to be with their dad.

We all spent several days together; Bill was now wearing an "ankle bracelet" and wasn't allowed to go too far from home. As always, the kids and I promised to do whatever we could to support him. It ripped my heart out to watch Cory and Kinsey say good bye to their dad; they tearfully told him how much they loved and supported him. Three weeks later I, along with my sister and a friend, drove Bill to prison. That was an agonizing and surreal day. It was a 6 ½ hour drive to the federal prison and I felt like I couldn't breathe most of the way.

The drive was endless, and when we finally pulled up to the stark, cement block prison, I walked with Bill to the entrance. There was a man in a prison jumpsuit pulling weeds. He watched us, smiled and said, "Hi," as we walked by him. He didn't have any teeth.

At the time, I wondered if they had been knocked out by another prisoner or the food and medical care was so bad that they fell out. Once we walked in the door, we were met by a guard. I had written Bill a letter to read after I left. I wanted him to know we would make it through this and that I was with him all the way. When I gave Bill the letter, the guard abruptly said no letters could be given to the prisoners. Hearing the word "prisoner" took me over the edge and I burst into tears. I pleaded with him to let Bill have my letter. The guard finally agreed; I'm sure he just wanted me to leave.

The ride home was as endless as the ride there. I laid down in the back seat and cried most of the way. I felt like I was watching a drama and that this certainly couldn't be "me" going through this. Plus, I had no idea how I was going to be able to manage things with Bill in prison.

Everything moved so fast that we didn't have much time to figure out expenses, but I knew that all Bill's insurance premiums from his business went into a joint account. Bill assured me that this money would be enough to live on until we could get him out of prison. My mind ached. I arrived home very late that night.

When I walked into the cold, dark house I felt so alone. Something told me this was going to be a very long and hard journey. I crawled, exhausted, up the stairs to bed. I pleaded,

"God, if You are real, I need You to show up now because I'm not sure I can do this alone."

I stumbled into bed and had my first of many, sleepless nights.

5

IMPENDING DOOM

The next three months were surreal and I felt like I was hanging on by a thread. The kids were in college. I was working part-time and trying to make ends meet. I picked up any extra consulting jobs I could to bring in additional money. Every spare moment was spent dealing with the IRS and a myriad of other financial issues.

I was deeply in debt and couldn't keep up with all my household bills, let alone the mounting attorney bills. Life was hard, crushing and exhausting. I hated being in the house alone and would stay out late either working or visiting friends to avoid being there. I drove the 6 ½ hour drive every weekend to visit Bill. Many weekends Cory drove 10 hours up from the University of Georgia and stayed with me – a huge comfort. Kinsey stayed at Indiana University only because she did not have a car.

When I visited Bill, I stayed at what I called the prison motel. As I remember, it was $17 a night - and that was highly overpriced. It was drab. It had a single small window in the back. There was one bare light bulb in the center of the ceiling and a lamp on a dresser. The lamp shade had caught on fire and all that was left was the wire frame; it had never been replaced.

The hotel was for women visiting men in prison and for local prostitutes. I was convinced it was run by retired prison guards. I seldom got towels. My room was rarely cleaned. In fact, cleaning was done only if the room was picked up and everything was off the floor. I just never seemed to pass the "clean test" and would get a nasty note about how I had left my socks on the floor or didn't put something away in my suitcase.

It took too much energy to fight all this. I grew used to pulling the sheets off the bed to use them as a towel, knowing I would never get any more towels or cleaning because the room was really a mess. There was no phone in the room and at that time, I couldn't afford a cell phone. The water faucet for the shower head was on the far side of the tub.

When you turned it on, ice cold water poured down from the shower head (there was no lever to get the water to come out of the faucet).

I always felt there were cameras in the room and people were secretly watching all of this and laughing. Men lingered outside drinking late into the night. One night I thought someone was being beaten to a pulp. The screams were deafening and terrifying. I had to make a decision to ignore them or risk walking outside by all the men to ask for help at the office. When I couldn't take the screaming any longer, I ran to the office in a panic telling them that a woman was being beaten and needed help.

The man at the desk showed no reaction; he didn't care and there was no way he was calling for help. I said I needed to have a phone in the room; I figured I could make the call. He proceeded to pull out a cardboard box of phones that looked like they were from the 1950s, bright turquoise, red, green, etc. He told me that I would have to pay to get one; getting a phone cost as much as the room. I left without a phone and was unable to get help for that poor woman.

I reduced myself to bringing the front desk staff candy so they would let me stay by the office versus the far side of the motel, which was down a hill and very isolated. I'm not sure the room by the office afforded much security, but I had fewer drunk men to walk by to get to my car.

After a grueling week and a long drive, I was usually at the end of my rope by the time I arrived at the prison motel. When I arrived one Friday around 6 p.m. someone had just painted the door to my room. I was wearing a new sweater (a very big deal at that time) and when I pushed open the door in with my arms loaded with luggage and groceries, I got wet paint all over my new sweater. I went to the office to tell them about this and proceeded to be yelled at for messing up their paint job.

A maintenance man was immediately sent down to re-paint the door. My sweater was ruined, I had no energy to fight and I was reduced to tears. As I sat on the floor of the motel sobbing, I thought,

"What has happened to my life?"

My beautiful life with the proverbial two kids, house and white picket fence was, by now, a distant memory. And, I wanted it back.

During this time, as you can imagine, I was in survival mode. I worked all week, picked up extra jobs wherever I could, stayed out late at night, wrote Bill a letter most every night, drove to prison each weekend, and then started over the next week.

I continually checked in with Cory and Kinsey. I tried to protect them as much as possible from what was going on and I imagine they did the same for me. We talked often and for long periods of time. These phone conversations were the bright spots in my day. I also found myself having long conversations with God late into the night. These conversations were pretty raw and I poured out my anger, confusion, fear, or whatever I was experiencing at the time.

The pastor at church said that God already knows how we feel so there is no need to try to hide anything. This was a great relief. I said exactly what I felt and didn't worry that God would walk away. I wanted to be strong and have faith but didn't feel like I was pulling it off very well. I asked God to give me the strength to make it through the next day, and many times, just the next hour.

Visiting Bill in prison was grim. Of course, it all started with the long drive and then the aggravation of the prison motel. The visitation check-in procedure at prison took forever. There would be a long line of (mostly) women at the start of visiting hours. They always seemed to have the same man doing check-in. He moved painfully slow. Each person's name, address, ID etc. had to be entered into the computer. He typed with one finger.

Once my information was entered, the guards searched my purse. Everyone had to bring a clear plastic purse (like the one I had when I was five years old) to prison. It was a long wait before I was cleared to enter the visiting room. I sat down until each prisoner was brought up, one at a time. I remember not being able to catch my breath the first time I saw Bill in a prison jumpsuit with his number on the front. I never got used to this.

After an initial greeting, no physical contact with the prisoners was allowed and we were all in one large room. The smell from the many vending machines was nauseating. There were 100 people in the room on any given day and the big event was to get something out of the vending machine and cook it in the microwave. Long hours were spent trying to pass the time. People sat at tables right next to us or at our table on crowded days. It was loud and we had difficulty talking and hearing each other.

After a few hours there was not much left to say. But, I always stayed until the guards closed visiting hours. Then it was another night at the prison motel before starting the whole process over the next day. Late Sunday afternoon I left for the long drive home. I always had a liter of pop with me so I wouldn't fall asleep.

After about three months of weekly visits, there was an incident at prison, which ended with Bill being put in solitary confinement. During a visit he put his arm around me which was against the rules. The kids and I were sitting at a table and all of the sudden four prison guards came rushing up and put handcuffs on him and marched him out of the visiting room. This was unexpected and we were very frightened for Bill. We had no idea what was going on or why he was being cuffed and led away.

Cory was quiet and Kinsey was hysterical. We were told to leave immediately and the guards said that we would not be able to see Bill for the rest of the weekend. We went back to the motel room exhausted. There was the usual fighting and screaming going on in the room next to us. I didn't know how much more of this I could handle. I asked the kids to join hands and be in unity while I prayed.

Our life was rapidly deteriorating and I asked God to show us what was going on. Things were not making sense; I asked Him to let the total truth about everything come out. I also asked God to arrange it so we could see Bill the next day. The fighting and screaming continued for many more hours. It was a long night. The next day we went to the prison, though we had been told we would not be able to see Bill. God answered my prayer and the guards let us go down through the mass of barbed wire to solitary confinement where we were body searched and seated in a very small room that had a little door set in the big door.

Bill was escorted in handcuffs to our small room. He walked in and the big door slammed shut. Then the little door opened up and Bill was told to turn his back to the door and put his hands through the small door. Once he did this, the guard unlocked his handcuffs, removed them and then slammed the small door shut.

It was devastating for Cory, Kinsey and me to watch all of this. This same "handcuff procedure" took place when he had to go to the bathroom. Bill was happy to have our company but his focus was clearly on himself and not on how this was impacting us. We spent most of the day in this very small room. There was nothing to eat and the day was excruciating. This was the last time we visited Bill in prison.

6

THE TRUTH

When I prayed in the prison motel, asking God to let the total truth come out, I sure didn't know what I was in for. Two weeks after my prayer on December 23, the day-long teambuilding program at work that I was to lead got cancelled, which was very unusual. I called a good friend and told her my day had unexpectedly freed up and asked if she would go to lunch with me. She hesitated, surprised by my call and finally said, "Yes." She asked if she could pick me up a little early. I agreed.

What I didn't know was that this good friend and her husband, an attorney, had obtained a copy of the transcript from Bill's trial, which I hadn't attended. What she read had been so upsetting to her, that she made an appointment with our pastor to get some counsel on what to do. The pastor had told her God would show her what to do. Less than 24 hours after her meeting with the pastor, I called her for lunch.

This was a rough time for my kids and me. Christmas was two days away and our family had never been separated for this special holiday. I was feeling very low when she picked me up for lunch. I was looking for encouragement and support. Instead, when I got in the car, she immediately asked me:

"Do you want to know the truth about Bill, even if it really hurts?"

I didn't need to think about this for long before saying, "Yes." She then handed me the court transcript of the trial, the one I thought was a hearing and didn't attend. She said, "Read this" and was silent as I read the transcript and felt a wrenching pain like nothing I had ever experienced.

I read Bill's words as he confessed that he had lied to his family and had stolen, and spent, $1,000,000 from his aunt's trust fund. It was obvious he confessed at the trial to get a reduced prison sentence. I was numb and in shock. I couldn't breathe and felt like I was going to be sick. I had asked God for the "total truth" but had never dreamed that the truth would be so painful. How could my husband and best friend, whom I had known since I was five, be a liar, a thief and a convicted felon? It was excruciating.

I remember years earlier watching the movie, *City Slickers,* when the three men riding horses each shared the worst day of his life. Each could pinpoint in vivid detail what had taken place on his worst day. Well, reading that transcript was the worst *moment* of my life.

My world imploded. The truth was staring me in the face. The betrayal was crushing, and I knew right then everything had changed. I thanked my friend for her courage in showing me this. As my friend and I ate bowls of soup in the midst of people joyously celebrating Christmas, as low as I felt, I had no idea there would be more to come as my world unraveled.

My friend dropped me off at the office and we hugged each other before I went in. Somehow I managed to finish the day at work. I then had to go home and "enjoy" a very special (day before) Christmas Eve dinner. My mom and dad had come up from Florida to spend Christmas with Cory, Kinsey and me.

I wasn't sure I could manage any Christmas cheer as I choked down my mom's carefully prepared turkey dinner. I was determined not to spoil another evening with the kids, and I certainly didn't want to alarm my parents.

The truth could wait one more day. Bill called from prison during dinner and, of course, talked with everyone. I got through my conversation with him as quickly as possible, and handed off the phone to the kids who were anxious and delighted to talk with him.

Anger, fear and resentment raced through my mind as we opened our Christmas gifts. I couldn't wait to tuck the kids into bed so I could be alone to figure out my next steps. My heart broke for what I knew I had to tell Cory and Kinsey.

The next morning my parents drove to my sister's house three hours south of us. The kids and I were to drive down later that day so the whole family could be together for Christmas Eve. I let them wake up on their own. I felt sick as I fixed them breakfast.

Once they finished, I sat them down and said I had something very difficult to share with them. I asked them to join hands with me and then asked God for strength and unity. The color quickly drained out of their faces. I then gave each of them a copy of the court transcript to read. The silence in the room was deafening. If I had thought it was hard to read Bill's words myself, it was ten times more difficult to watch the two people I loved most in the world experience the same sense of betrayal.

They were in shock. We tried to comprehend it all. We loved Bill and couldn't imagine he was capable of stealing and lying to us. Our heads were spinning, the pain was so intense. And, we only had a few hours before we had to drive down to celebrate Christmas Eve with the whole family.

On the way to my sister's house, we stopped to make copies of the court transcript for each family member. When we arrived, my sister's beautifully decorated house was filled with laughter and the smell of turkey and all the fixings. The three of us choked down another Christmas dinner and opened gifts.

After the celebration ended, I told everyone I had something they needed to read. It was important that this message was delivered in person to all the family members who had traveled to be together. Once again, the three of us had to watch the painful reactions as my parents, sister, brother-in-law, cousins and extended family all read the transcript.

The fun evening turned somber. The air was sucked out of the room as each family member dealt with the shocking news. I felt a wave of exhaustion encompassing me and couldn't wait to get to bed. The three of us went upstairs and tried to get some sleep before heading down to Florida the next morning. This was a planned trip to spend a few days in the sun with my parents who were flying down the next day. The kids and I rose very early on Christmas morning to head south. As expected, traffic was light. We made it to Georgia the first night and slept at Cory's apartment at the University of Georgia. Our Christmas dinner that night was a jar of Ragu spaghetti.

The next day, we arrived, exhausted, in Florida. We waited for Bill to call. Once again, I prayed with the kids for strength and for the right words to come. I wanted to be mindful, present and deliberate when I talked with him. He called the next evening. I was amazed at how much peace God gave me for this dreaded conversation.

I was the first to talk to Bill and was very composed as I told him we knew the truth. I told him we had read the transcript and knew he had lied and had stolen $1,000,000. There was silence on the other end. Bill's voice was shaking as he apologized and said,

"But I only told one lie."

I calmly replied, "No, you have lied every day to your family for a long time. Your actions sold us out for years, and you could have gone to prison at any time."

By this time, Bill was crying and begging me to forgive him. My last words to him were,

"I don't know what will happen to us, but this journey is yours alone to take. No one can help you."

I added that I would not be having any more contact with him. I then let Cory and Kinsey have their own conversations with him. I walked into another room and don't know what was said in their conversations.

The next day I contacted Bill's parents who lived in Naples, Florida. Although we hadn't communicated with them for five years, I felt we needed to see them in person and share the transcript with them. We drove two hours to their house and I was surprised they ran out to warmly greet us; I hadn't been sure how they would receive us after the years of no communication.

After a few pleasantries, I gave them the court transcript to read. Cory, Kinsey and I watched their distraught faces as they read about their son and could feel their pain. Although Bill's parents were heartbroken, they thanked us profusely for making the trip to Naples to see them. Once again, it was a long, hard day.

We spent a few more days in Florida. It was healing

to walk along the beach. But this respite ended quickly; Kinsey and Cory had to return to school and I went back to Toledo. Saying goodbye to the kids was excruciating. I knew trauma could either bind a family together, or tear them apart. I hated the thought of us being so far away from each other.

I arrived in Toledo on New Year's Day. It was bleak and frigid. My mood matched the weather. I soon embarked on a journey to make sense of my marriage. My parents and siblings did not live in town so much of this journey had to be taken alone.

It was during this time that I learned to rely on God to get me through whatever came my way each day. He was my hope, my confidant and my counselor. I desperately needed Him, but at the same time, wasn't so sure I wanted a relationship with a God who could allow this to happen.

7

CRUSHED DREAMS

Hope is powerful. It was hope that got me through the pain and loss of the past few years. Our family was close and strong. While I'd had confidence we would eventually get through all the problems and be united again, it was clear that dream was dead. I had to accept the brutal truth – and it was brutal - that Bill had lied to us over and over again. He had put our family at great risk for many years. Furthermore, he had never really taken responsibility for all that he had done.

Living with hope had been hard, but living without the hope of a united family was overwhelming. I desperately needed God, but I also realized I was mad at Him. He knew the most important thing in the world to me was family, so why was He allowing this dream along with so many others, to be crushed? I was devastated and felt so alone.

I didn't have too much time to dwell on my crushed dreams because life moved forward with a vengeance. Almost immediately, after my return from Florida, I had to deal with a series of floods in the house. First the basement flooded and then the base of a large plant leaked green water, which stained and ruined a good portion of the living room carpet. In the midst of dealing with all of that, there was a leak upstairs and water was pouring down into the kitchen.

Finally, the dishwasher flooded and did much water damage to the wood floor. I didn't know how to deal with all these floods and had very little money to get help. When I look back on this time, I have to wonder if all these floods were symbolic of what was happening in my life: I was underwater and needed help fast.

During this time, I received lots of calls from people, many of whom I did not know, telling me that Bill owed them money. These calls were threatening, and the expectation was that I would pay them off. One of the worst experiences happened when I was sitting in the kitchen late one night. All of the sudden a strange man was pounding on the kitchen window yelling that I needed to get him money that Bill owed him, right now. I didn't know the man and ran upstairs. I no longer felt safe or secure in the house and wondered how many other people would show up demanding payment.

As I came to grips with the depth of Bill's betrayal, it dawned on me that there were probably many other areas where he also lied. And, I was right. It seemed like every day I got more bad news, either by phone or in the mail. Unpaid bills arrived, creditors, and random people all wanted money. I was also dealing with the IRS because we had always filed joint returns. The tax fraud that landed Bill in prison was due to unclaimed income, which was the million dollars he had stolen.

Under the law, I was liable for this unless I could be declared an innocent spouse, which was extremely difficult to do. Dealing with the IRS was terrifying. Our returns were complicated because Bill owned his own business, and it was hard for me to make sense of them. One day I got a notice in the mail that I was being sued by a bank. Turns out, Bill had borrowed $200,000 from this bank a few months before going to prison and my name had been forged on the loan papers. I quickly realized you don't just tell a bank, "This is all a big mistake," when they are suing you. You need to get an attorney and fight things through. This happened many times for many different situations. I found out a deposition was given in my name and I knew nothing about it. I was also told someone had impersonated me in a court case. Bill owned a life insurance company but had forged my name to collect the cash value from my life insurance policy. He also cashed in and took the money from the children's policies.

Now that Bill wasn't in town to do damage control, the house of cards fell quickly. The bad news kept coming. I was rapidly going under. One day I added up my attorney bills connected with Bill's theft and they were $70,000, which was more than my gross income. I had never thought much about money before because I had always had plenty. Now I was forced to think about money all the time. All those floods seemed to foretell my own situation: I was sinking, or maybe, had sunk.

One of the most repugnant things I had to do was to constantly try to prove to the IRS, attorneys, banks and individuals that I wasn't a criminal. These creditors had much to gain if I had been in cahoots with Bill; it would enable them to get money from me and garnish my wages. I hated trying to prove over and over again that I was honest. It was demeaning and wearing. I thought I would get used to this in time and it wouldn't bother me as much.

The truth was it bothered me more with every encounter. I realized this when someone once questioned an item on a work expense account and I practically bit off their head. Though, I went to them the next day and apologized, it was clear I was under tremendous strain.

Although the money issues were huge, they paled in comparison to the worries I had about the children. Cory and Kinsey each handled this trauma very differently. Cory directed his energies to excel and get excellent grades at college. He had decided he wanted to become a lawyer and knew the competition to get in a top school would be intense. Though I was concerned that anger was fueling his drive, I decided that maybe this wasn't such a bad thing. Cory called often and could not have been more supportive and protective of me.

Kinsey's reaction was different. She was getting depressed. I suspected she was not attending her classes at Indiana University, and this proved to be the case. Her father's betrayal had sunk her into a deep hole. Unlike Cory, Kinsey had made a decision that she wanted to keep in contact with Bill. I was very concerned about this but knew I had to let her work through her own relationship with her father.

Later, I found out that Bill had been calling her many times each day. He told Kinsey she was his only link to life outside of prison and he leaned heavily on her for support. This broke my heart but I knew I only had so much influence over my 18-year-old. I became increasingly worried about her and tried to visit her at college as often as possible.

Kinsey and I made an agreement that she would call when she was getting ready for bed, about 11 p.m., and I would talk with her until she fell asleep. She would drop off mid-sentence anywhere from 1 to 2 a.m. Although these late hours were exhausting, it was a comfort to know what was on her mind. These nights, I only got several hours of sleep before training a room full of adults the next day at work. It was only through God's grace that I didn't get sick during those months.

Kinsey's issues were far beyond sleep and school. I became suspicious she was dating abusive men. When I asked her about this she said, "If my dad didn't care for me, how could anyone else?"

I learned, much later, that she had been running in front of cars hoping she would be hit and killed. Desperate to help her, I went to the free counseling center at a nearby university and asked what I should do: I had wanted her to come home, but she wouldn't. I had prayed that God would give me a counselor who would give me sound advice. This one told me that Kinsey had been controlled much of her life by her dad and was now being controlled by abusive men.

The counselor told me that because I was the one person, along with her brother, that she totally trusted, the worst thing I could do was try to control her by bringing her home. That night I had a major "heart-to-heart" with God.

I screamed, cried and yelled and said He could NOT let anything happen to her or Cory. If anything happened to them, I would be finished. I knew I had to totally trust God to watch over them. My conversation with God was filled with fear, pain and anger. I had little peace and I begged Him every night to protect my children. All of this chaos made my life very lonely.

Many people did not know what was going on, and I said very little. Those who knew the situation didn't know how to help. I understood why people were uncomfortable. Because of this experience, I made a decision that I would always go directly to people in pain and ask how they were doing, and then respect it if they wanted privacy. I also learned that when well-intentioned people asked what I needed, I didn't even know where to begin.

I was always so thankful when someone just did something. I talked to God a lot during this time and appreciated that He was available 24/7 and at no cost. Some days I felt very close to Him and other days I wondered if He was even there. We had an up and down relationship and I would soon be putting God to the test.

8

THE TEST

Things were quickly going from bad to worse and I suspected that I would soon lose everything. When I compared my income to my expenses, the only question I had was, "How much longer can I hang on?"

One Sunday, my pastor gave a sermon on the book of Malachi (Chapter 3). He was talking about tithing, giving 10 percent of your income back to the church, and said this is the only place in the Bible where God invites people to test Him. I listened intently. The pastor continued, saying that God tells us to pay our tithes and, in return, He will give us food for our house, rebuke the devourer, and pour out a blessing so large there would not be room enough to receive it. He reiterated that God invites us to test Him on this. What? Was he kidding? This just made me angry and on the way home, I yelled, "God, this is totally ridiculous!"

I was in debt up to my eyeballs, I was losing everything, I had a husband in prison and two kids in college. I screamed, "Okay, I will test You in this. But there is no way things will work out."

At that time I cared only about getting food in my house – I didn't even have enough money for groceries! I started tithing that day and was just waiting until the time when I could prove God wrong. To my amazement, this never happened.

During this time, I was getting a deeper understanding of what it means for God to "pour out a blessing." In the past I had always equated blessing with family, friends, health and material possessions. God does bless us with those things, but He gave me a new revelation of how real blessing comes when He transforms us by changing our hearts. I'm not sure how had I missed that concept during all my Sundays in church, but I had.

Now, though, I found the more I was willing to trust Him, the more He stepped in. And, there were plenty of opportunities for Him to step in because I was in way over my head and didn't have a clue how to manage things. God did keep food in my house and blessed me by changing my heart, a journey that I hope will continue for a lifetime.

One of the blessings I received was to learn who my friends are. When darkness comes, the light is very evident to see. Most all my friends stayed by my side and were so kind. They asked me to dinner and included me in their special family events. They also thought of fun adventures like a mystery evening that would include dinner, a massage and a movie.

Others planned a day of shopping where I was given $20 to spend at a second-hand clothes store. Each of us laughed so hard as we tried on outfits until we found the perfect one complete with shoes, jewelry and a handbag, all for under $20. Then we would wear our outfits out that night to a symphony or concert. I loved these adventures with my friends but their best gift was to listen to me when I needed to talk with someone. It was comforting to not have to be "on" and to be able to say whatever I wanted with them.

Along with my friends' kindness, I was touched to receive anonymous gifts. It wasn't uncommon to come home and find a few bags of groceries on my porch. And, as much as I disliked getting the mail, because I continued to receive bad news, on any given day there would be $20 or $50 in the mailbox.

I also found books or plants by my front door with a card that said, "God loves you."

These gifts prompted me to start thinking of all the people who could have been responsible and it made me look at each one of my friends and wonder,

"Was it you?"

Every gift felt like it had 100 possible donors. Very cool! I vowed at the time that I would become the best anonymous gift giver, if I could ever get back on my feet. Life was still rough, but all these acts of kindness profoundly impacted me by showing me how much people really cared.

As always, my family stayed right by my side. My parents, sister and her husband could not have been better; I would not have made it through without them. Even though they weren't in town, I always knew they were there for me. For example, my car died shortly after Bill went to prison and I had no money to buy a new one. My sister's husband immediately offered to give me one of his cars to use. This was a lifesaver because I traveled a lot for my job.

Cory and Kinsey were unbelievable; in the midst of their pain, they tried to protect and comfort me when I was the one who should have been their protector and comforter. They were attentive to me as well as to each other and we stayed in very close contact. They gave me strength and were my incentive to never give up.

Despite the generosity of my friends and family members, my financial situation continued to go downhill. Bill was becoming increasingly angry and sent hurtful letters to the family. All of this made it easy to get sympathy if I wanted it because the few people who knew what was going on felt sorry for me. One, however, also challenged me.

I was at her house after another major incident with Bill and as I was telling her what had happened, she picked up my purse and threw it as hard as she could into the wall. All the contents rolled out on the floor, breaking some of them.

"Why did you do that?" I asked, shocked.

She answered – and I'll never forget this, "You see your purse in the corner with all the broken stuff on the floor? That is Bill. He is in prison and he's broken, just like your stuff. I'm sick of hearing about Bill. It's no longer about him but about you. How are you going to walk through this?"

There it was, the ton of bricks I needed to get moving. But, not recognizing it for the gift it was, I went home deeply offended. After a good cry, though, I realized she was right. It was now about me. How was I going to handle all of this? I wanted to walk through it with strength and dignity. I had to for myself and for my children.

Someone had recently given me the book, *The Bait of Satan*, which argues that the bait is offense. If Satan can get us to think about how bad our life is, we begin to expect others to do more to help out, which starts us on a rapid downhill spiral. This incident shook me to the core. I didn't want Bill's drama to define me. I had heard people say that your witness is your walk, and I wanted to be a good witness for God. So, I asked God for help. I also joined the intercessory prayer team at church to force me to think of and pray for others rather than focusing on just myself. This was a big help.

As I was learning to lean on God, I continued to find out more about Bill's criminal activity. It didn't shock me. Frankly, so much had already happened and I was too numb to be shocked. It seemed like everything I felt could never possibly happen, had happened, so what was one more thing? I had to think through how to handle all this with Cory and Kinsey. I decided to call them and ask them a question:

"Do you want to be treated as adults or children as we walk through everything with your Dad?"

I added, "I know it's very tempting to say you want to be treated as an adult, but if you make this decision, I will be forced to tell you things about your father that will break your heart."

I asked them to think about this for a week and then get back with me with an answer. I told them I would honor their decisions. Within a week both Cory and Kinsey called and said they wanted to be treated as adults. I would have respected whatever they said, but this allowed the three of us to be partners as we began to unravel our life with Bill.

I realized I needed to make another major decision. As I learned more about Bill's life, I started to think about divorce. This was a word, along with "prison," that had not been a part of my vocabulary. Marriage was a lifetime covenant and I secretly hoped that God would bring Bill to his knees so that he would own his actions and repent. I wanted God to heal him so we could restore our life. But what I was seeing made this hope seem impossible.

By this time, I was becoming more used to God answering my questions and leading me. I knew it said in Proverbs 3:5-6:

"Trust in the Lord with all your heart, and lean not on your own understanding. In all your ways acknowledge Him, and He will direct your paths."

I trusted God to lead me and He did, even when it came to divorce. But, His leading, like my request for the whole truth about Bill, came in a very unexpected way that kicked off a whole new series of events.

9

DIVORCE

Like most women, I believed marriage was forever. Though, I certainly knew plenty of people who were divorced, I had decided that would never be my reality. Bill and I were so close. Best friends, really. This question of whether to divorce Bill plagued me and I needed resolution. One night after doing an out-of-town training class for work, I got on my knees in my hotel room and pleaded with God, asking,

"What should I do?"

I added, "You hate divorce and so do I. Furthermore, though You can change Bill's heart, it doesn't look like You are going to do that."

I was feeling pretty desperate and reminded God that He promised to direct our paths. I said,

"Give me a sign, one that I cannot miss. I need to know what to do."

And, I told Him that I was going to stop eating until I received His sign; I wanted to be sure God knew how serious I was about this important decision.

I drove back home the next day and went right into the office. When I checked my voicemail, there was a message to call my bank immediately. I was perplexed and called right away. I was told that I was way overdrawn on my account. What?

"Impossible," I told them. "I'm always very careful."

The manager clued me in, and I was stunned. Turns out, Bill had called the bank from prison and had my name removed from our joint account, which held his insurance premiums, the same account I counted on to make it through this tough time. I'm sure it wasn't even legal for him to remove my name, but I had no money, energy or time to fight another battle.

With resignation, I realized that God had given me my "sign." I trembled when I grasped the enormity of what Bill had done – by cutting off my money supply, for all he knew, he put us, his family "out on the street."

I remember saying to God, "Hey, You didn't need to give that big of a sign."

But I quickly remembered I had asked Him to make it big enough I couldn't miss it. As painful as this was, it was now very clear: I would seek a divorce. I remember pulling the phone book out of my desk and opening it up to divorce attorneys in the yellow pages. I asked God to help me get a good attorney, then shut my eyes, and let my finger land on the page. With total resignation, I called that attorney and when she answered, I flatly said,

"I need to get a divorce."

This was something I thought would never happen to me. Now, my hope of having a united family had been officially crushed. Then, as had happened so many times before, I had to first deal with my own pain and then watch the pain on my children's faces as I told them what had transpired.

They, as I was, were incredulous. I was happy they had asked to be treated as adults so I didn't have to sugarcoat anything. It was what it was. Bill, who was supposed to be our protector and provider, had cut off our key supply of money. We were beginning to realize we didn't even know him.

Bill was served divorce papers in prison. Because I was spending a lot of time doing the required paperwork for our divorce, and because I was asked to document Bill's criminal activity that had never been exposed in the trial, I asked God to give me someone to help. I never got any help. However, I now believe God wanted to be sure I saw and recorded all that had taken place, so I would be very clear and confident about moving ahead without Bill.

Bill was still in prison when I went to court to get the divorce. As always, the kids were right by my side and my sister, too, so she could be a key witness in the proceedings. By this time much had been uncovered and the charges against Bill were gross neglect of duty, extreme cruelty and embezzlement.

The divorce was granted and I was awarded $10,000 per month for life. I knew I would never see a penny of this – and I never have. I was numb at the trial and accepted the divorce was necessary. The next day the kids and I took at walk at a park and I tossed my wedding ring into the creek. They questioned me saying I could have sold it.

"I don't want any money for this ring because it isn't worth anything to me," I told them.

That might not have been the most prudent thing to do, but I've never had any regrets. Maybe God will orchestrate someone who needs a gift to find it; that would make me happy.

In the midst of preparing for the divorce came another series of events. Once I had no access to the bank account, I could no longer afford the rent on the house, so it was put on the market and, six months later, it was sold. Next I had to deal with the contents of the house. Thank goodness Kinsey was home at the time and took charge of working with the auctioneer. She was a tremendous help; I was so grateful I did not have to deal with this task.

Kinsey knew my most valuable possessions in the house were all the scrapbooks and family pictures, and that, as far as I was concerned, everything else could go. I had tried to protect my parents, who spent most of the year in Florida, from what was going on. I didn't want this drama to take away from their retirement, which they were enjoying so much. But now I had to tell them what was happening. Their response was amazing: "You can move in with us." they offered.

Their "summer house" was only two doors down from mine. What a relief to have a place to go, but it also dawned on me how close I was to being homeless. I was blessed to have a safety net with my family but also sobered to realize how many do not have this and find themselves on the streets.

I believe my final material breaking point came when I lost my favorite place in the world: my beloved cottage that had been bequeathed to me by a favorite uncle. I loved that cottage on Fire Island in New York and our family enjoyed many wonderful vacations there. It is a beautiful and peaceful island, with the Great South Bay on one side and the Atlantic Ocean on the other. I had hoped when Cory and Kinsey had children of their own, they could create more wonderful memories.

Years earlier, I had put the cottage in a trust for them so they would own it when they were 30 years old. Although there were no strings attached and they could have sold the cottage, I had secretly hoped the cottage would be a link to bond their families together.

I had heard the question, "Do you own your possessions or do they own you?"

Well, when I looked back, I realize my cottage on Fire Island had definitely owned me. But since there was now no way I could ever buy it back from my parents, it was sold within a few months. Something broke in me when it was sold and I no longer cared much about material possessions.

As weird as it sounds, I even felt kind of free when all my house possessions were sold. It wasn't nearly as hard as I thought it would be. Once again, I know that was God's grace. I no longer had security in things, but was getting more and more security in Him.

I continued to get new revelations about life. For example, though I was relieved when my possessions were sold, 1 learned how easy it is to take advantage of people when they are vulnerable. Many things happened to me and the children that were wrong, and I remember several people challenging me by asking, "What are you going to do, sue me?"

They knew I didn't have the money to get an attorney to fight things, so it gave them leeway to exploit me. This happened when the contents of our house were sold. We had a four-bedroom house: furnished basement, attic, living room, dining room, family room and large kitchen. Bill and I had been given many nice wedding presents including, silver, china, art objects and signed glass.

When the final settlement came for all the contents of the house, I received a check for $425. I had expected much more than that and was going to use it to pay off bills. Once again, I didn't have the money to get an attorney to fight back, so I let it go.

I remember calling the kids and saying,

"Never sacrifice your family over material possessions, because they aren't worth much anyway."

But, to this day, I get livid if I see someone taking advantage of someone who can't fight back. Maybe I'll do more about this when my work schedule isn't so demanding.

I also became aware of how differently I was treated in the courts when I was married to Bill, a "successful" business owner, versus when I was a broke single mother. This treatment was not overt but was shown in much more subtle ways such as the warmth of a greeting, tone of voice, poor listening and a dismissive attitude toward my ideas.

The respect shown to Bill and me throughout our lives had been invisible to me and I would have argued vehemently if someone had told me they didn't receive the same respect. I guess I had to experience this discrimination to believe it.

Additionally, in the past when I saw someone financially struggling I would have thought to myself,

"They need to work harder, like I have, then they could get out of their situation."

Well, I had never worked harder in my life during this time and was losing ground fast. As a result, I learned to show much more respect and have more empathy for those in poverty. I also gained great compassion for people going through tough times.

Though each of these new experiences was difficult to walk through, I knew I was becoming a richer, deeper person in the process. And, I liked who I was becoming!

Although God was teaching me much and leading me, I had a tender spot in my heart that was causing continual pain, and that spot had to do with forgiveness. Many of my Christian friends had told me I needed to forgive Bill. Were they out of their minds? I had been fighting battles for the past year while he sat in prison with three square meals a day and lots of free time. And, I was supposed to forgive him! What were they thinking? And had they ever faced this kind of betrayal? If they had walked in my shoes, I could have listened to them, but frankly they just made me angry. I felt they were out of touch with reality.

Still, I was very aware I had experienced much torment, during those few hours of sleep I managed to get each night. I replayed incidents, wondered why I hadn't seen who Bill really was, worried about new problems and then became so worked up that I was unable to sleep. I even went to the local bookstores, sat on the small stools, and read books on forgiveness; I didn't have the money to actually buy any books.

None of this gave me much relief and I began to feel like a failure because as hard as I tried, I was unable to let go of what Bill had done. I knew this could become a big stumbling block. God did intervene, but it came in a way that I could have never expected.

10

FORGIVENESS

Several weeks later, I was at church on a Thursday evening. I always liked going to church because I felt safe and at peace there. During praise and worship, one of my favorite parts of the service, a woman I knew from a church class was standing next to me. Because we'd been in class together, I knew she lived on the streets, was a crack addict and had prostituted herself and stolen to support her habit. She also knew a little about what was going on with me.

Right in the middle of a song, she looked at me and said quite loudly, "I can see that you're doing time with your husband."

I turned to her in disbelief and said, "What did you just say?"

I was mad at what she said and also because she was interfering with the peace I longed for during worship. The woman answered very matter-of-factly, "I can see you're doing time with your husband. You are holding the keys of unforgiveness so tight you might as well be doing guard duty in the prison with him."

Now I was really mad and replied, "You know, it's not that easy!"

The woman didn't miss a beat, as she looked at me with a measure of disgust and answered, "Why don't you ask God to help you?"

I was offended. Though I made it through the rest of the service, I went home for a long cry. Deep down, I knew a homeless crack addict had given me one of the best pieces of wisdom I had ever received. That night, I humbled myself, got down on my knees and begged God to help me to forgive Bill and to end the nightly torment. I didn't receive immediate relief, but I got some.

Within three months I was able to sleep, and within a year, peace replaced the torment. My anger was replaced by sadness for my husband, who had lost so much. By that time, I was able to write my only letter to Bill since we had divorced. I told him I had forgiven him, and although I still wanted no contact, I hoped he would be able to move on and have a good life.

You know, I had read so many books on forgiveness, but they seemed academic and long to me. I couldn't relate to any of them. Someday I will write my own book on forgiveness and it will contain only two sentences:

1. <u>Forgiveness is a choice</u>. I came to understand the first and biggest step was for me to sincerely want to forgive Bill. That might sound easy, but it wasn't. I realized a part of me wanted to hang onto the pain. I'm not sure why; maybe because I could get some sympathy any time I wanted or I could continue to talk about the terrible things Bill had done. I knew if I forgave Bill, then I would no longer be able to talk about him. It took me a while to decide if I really wanted to do this. It felt like a huge responsibility.

2. <u>Even if you want to forgive, you probably aren't strong enough to forgive without God's help and grace.</u> The first sentence of my short book on forgiveness was much harder than the second sentence. I had been through enough fires at this point to know that I couldn't do much of anything without God's help. I believe once God knew I was

>genuine about wanting to let go of the hurt,
>then He stepped in and did the rest.

The time following our divorce continued to be a time of reflection. One thing I mulled over and over was the advice I had received from my good friend when she threw my purse into the wall, and said,

"How are *you* going to walk through this journey?"

After much thought, I made a decision to pray a very dangerous prayer. I asked God to show me who I really was, clean me up and change my heart. Although I was apprehensive about what was coming, I knew God would answer this prayer. It didn't take long for the answers to come.

Almost immediately, God brought up my pride. I heard no voice but His clear thoughts entered my heart and brain. I know they were His thoughts because I was taken aback. I knew I didn't see things the way He did.

He asked me, "Why didn't you ever ask for help?"

I answered, "I was pleased with myself because I was able to figure out most things on my own."

He quickly answered, "That was pride. The real truth is that you were too ashamed to let people, even your own family, know how bad things were. You stayed in a sleazy, unsafe prison motel instead of asking for help. You could have asked 100 different people to loan you $50 to stay in a decent hotel but you didn't because then they would know how down and out you were."

I weakly replied, "But I thought I was being resourceful."

God did not let me off the hook and clearly told me that this was my pride and independent spirit.

He went on to say, "You are used to being in control and you like it. You are always the giver and decide what you do and when to do it. Now you are out of control and must rely on others to give to you. This puts you in a position of no control."

He added, "Let people help you. They want to do this. Don't let your shame about the state you're in isolate you. We all need each other."

Wow, this was a total revelation to me! I had always been taught to be very independent and self sufficient; and this is good, to a point, but in my case it was clearly my pride that had kept me from asking for some much needed help. I never before realized how insidious pride is; not only was it invisible to me, but I was proud of my pride, in that I saw it as great resourcefulness.

I could see this journey of cleaning me up would not be as easy or as short as I had originally thought. The difference now was God and I were working together in this effort. And the clean-up continued.

I found God gave me messages when I least expected them. I was out for a walk one morning and God said I didn't really understand how to love. I was pretty indignant and told Him that "love" was one of the few things that I knew I was good at. I couldn't believe He was telling me this.

Once again, His "words" were as clear as a bell as He said, "I want you to learn to love like I love. I want your heart to break for what breaks Mine. You are far from that."

By this time I was getting better at this new partnership with God so I said, "OK, then You are going to have to show me how to love like You because I think I do pretty well in this area."

God followed through on that request; over time, He gently showed me how self-centered my love really was. I realized how I related everything to me and how it would impact me.

I also came to learn that trusting God meant to obey Him. It took some time to get this lesson down. I distinctly remember one day at church when God asked me to walk over and comfort a woman. I was to put my hand on her shoulder and say something encouraging. One of my kids was with me and I felt stupid going over to this woman I didn't know, so I didn't.

When I got in the car to go home, I felt terrible, because I knew I had let God down. This feeling lasted for a week before I asked Him to give me another chance. It wasn't too much longer before He did. Once again, I was at church and He told me to walk over to a woman and give her a hug and tell her that things would be okay. I felt uneasy about this but knew it would be much easier to do that than to suffer the remorse I had felt the last time.

After the service was over, I practically ran over to this woman and did exactly what He had asked. She immediately started crying and told me she had lost her job that day and didn't know how she was going to make it. Well, I knew all about this kind of loss.

We spent the next few hours talking and ended up becoming close friends. I realized God works through people and if I hadn't obeyed Him, He would have found someone else to comfort that woman and I would have missed out on helping her and gaining a good friend. I was surprised God was so involved in the little and practical things of life. I was looking for bigger and more dramatic stuff, but

God continued to put small things on my heart: like buying someone a certain book, giving a woman money in the grocery store parking lot, buying a stranger lunch, writing someone an encouraging note, etc.

I learned to trust what He was telling me and to respond at once. We became partners in this process. I was genuinely happy when He showed me an ugly root in my heart and then through His grace and mercy started the process of pulling it out. I found that I was almost disappointed when He wasn't showing me something and I no longer had any illusions about how far my heart and thinking were from His. I also came to appreciate that life with God was exciting; I never knew what He would think of next.

And, I was starting to enjoy letting go of the steering wheel and letting Him take over. I could see being in control was highly overrated. Maybe, this journey would be more fun than I had expected.

11

CLEAN UP

As part of my "clean up" I decided to get some counseling. My pastor at church had been wonderful and met with me often. I also started going to a second counselor. I needed to unravel the past 30 years of my marriage. I had known Bill since kindergarten and we had had an extraordinarily happy marriage.

As strange as it may seem, the kids and I adored him and we felt he also adored us. Life had been full and good. Our home was happy; we enjoyed being together and were close. Bill appeared to always be there for Cory, Kinsey and me. He supported us, made time to talk and be with us, took an active interest in what we did and was a big help around the house. He took his role as a father seriously. He coached the kids' sports teams, got to know their friends and planned many fun events for the four of us.

Bill was also a good neighbor and made a point to help people whether it was cleaning someone's gutters, moving furniture or helping them with yard work. Bill and I had many friends whom we enjoyed and traveled with on family vacations. So, who really was this man, and what didn't I see that had ultimately caused Cory, Kinsey, me and so many others such pain?

As it turned out, my counselor told me Bill was likely a sociopath. I'm not a psychologist but was told that a lack of conscience, narcissism, risk-taking, chronic lying and charisma are some of the traits of a sociopath. The "real" Bill exhibited those traits. I was told there's not a lot of information on sociopaths but they always feel they are the ones in the right, and therefore, believe they don't need to see a counselor.

Since Bill and I had gone to counseling off and on throughout our marriage, I thought, "Wow, what have I missed over the years?"

Were all those good deeds just Bill's way of assuaging his guilt, or was it a control issue? The hardest question for me to reconcile was, "Did Bill really love me and the children?"

The counselor gently told me that Bill probably didn't know what love was. He added,

"Bill loved you the same way he loved a piece of furniture or a movie. You were great camouflage, which enabled him to steal for many years and not be suspected."

I was crushed. Were the last 30 years of my life smoke and mirrors? Did it mean anything? Was I really handpicked, as the counselor said, to be only a good cover for Bill's criminal activity?

My job was in Human Resources and I had always thought myself perceptive about people. Was I in the wrong field at work? My self-esteem plummeted but I was determined to survive and to not let this define me. I would get through it somehow. The counselor said if I really wanted to heal, I needed to walk through my marriage with Bill, put it on a table, examine it, touch it, talk about it, and then place it on a shelf.

I was told I wouldn't forget it, but it wouldn't be front and center in my mind. I decided to walk out this journey. It was long, humbling and painful. The worst part was knowing how all of this impacted and could potentially continue to impact Cory and

Kinsey. Counseling helped me to see how complex humans are, that we are all a mix of good and evil. I wondered, "So how does someone get out of balance and move toward evil?"

True, I had forgiven Bill. Now God was showing me how many times He had forgiven me. I wondered if God needs evil in the world to show His goodness and mercy. I believe He does. I wondered if a person's heart can change, if so, how. I had tried for years to change my own heart and was unsuccessful. It didn't take me long to realize only God could do the deep work needed to heal and change hearts. And, I knew I had to ask Him to do this.

Why didn't I know this when I was 10? I went to church every Sunday but must not have paid very good attention. I've heard people say God doesn't do miracles like He used to in the Bible. My experience was He was doing the best and greatest miracle by changing my heart. Many might not consider this a miracle but I did and it meant everything to me.

It was strange to realize that though my heart had changed significantly, I felt I acted pretty much the same on the outside. For me, God worked from the inside out. First, He changed my heart, and then later, my actions. My thinking about so many things changed dramatically during this time. I wasn't the same person, yet only a few others were aware of how I'd changed.

While I was in counseling I had two surprises: one good and one bad. The good surprise was I received an unexpected check. I was astonished when I opened the mail one day and found a check for $16,000. Wow, I hadn't seen that much money in a long time. The check was from a mutual fund that somehow had been missed when I lost everything. I couldn't believe it! I wondered, if I should let the bank know about this because all the money was to be accounted for during this time, or if I should buy a car.

I had been driving my brother-in-law's car and when it needed to be sold others always offered me a car. I never had to ask to borrow one. I knew legally I was responsible for covering Bill's debts and had lost everything in doing so. I sought legal advice and didn't receive a clear answer so I asked God what to do. I wasn't certain of God's leading, but felt I was to use the money to get a car. I had no idea what to get but happened to watch an ad on TV for Saturn, which said the salespeople would not negotiate and the list price was the real price.

That sold me because I didn't think I could handle dealing with a car salesman. I wasn't sure what a

Saturn looked like but drove over to the dealership and to my surprise found that a new Saturn cost $16,000. I took that as a sign and bought the car.

I drove home a week later with my new car. I couldn't believe I finally had my own wheels! This was much more exciting than any car I had ever had. Once again, God provided for me in the most unexpected and delightful way. I loved my little Saturn and it lasted many years!

The second surprise was not a good one. I learned that Bill, who was still in prison, was contesting our divorce. I had to re-engage my attorney to fight this. I was getting sick of paying attorneys and being called in for depositions, which were upsetting, inconvenient and expensive. To make things worse, Bill would fire his attorneys after a few months and hire new ones, which forced me to repeat the series of depositions. After six months of this, the case finally went to trial.

To my astonishment, it was decided in Bill's favor! I was incredulous and thought surely there must be some mistake. My attorney said Bill had won the case, the divorce was overturned and I was once again married. I was shocked.

My attorney explained in the initial divorce decree the judge forgot to put in why I was receiving such a large monthly settlement: $10,000. Of course I had never received a penny but was told the judge needed to explain why this settlement was so big. It was due to Bill's financial misconduct.

I said, "Okay, that is easy enough, go add the sentence."

Unfortunately, the judge who presided over the original divorce had died and he was the only one who could alter our divorce decree. I couldn't believe what I was hearing and asked, "You mean Bill is in prison for tax fraud? But that doesn't constitute financial misconduct!"

Yes, that was the case. So after a year-and-a-half of depositions, hearings, trials and finally getting a divorce, I was back to square one and married again! I was furious. And to make matters worse, my attorney, for whom I had much respect, confided in me she had recently been diagnosed with cancer and would not be able to represent me in this new trial. I was sad for her, and just as sad for myself.

Now I would have to start all over in explaining this complex and messy story to a new attorney, all while the bills stacked up. God and I had a long talk that night. I reminded him I was still here and He could not forget about me because I would be needing lots of help.

It seemed like when I received good news, it would often be followed by bad news. I thought being close to God meant a more blessed life. This was confusing to me. Didn't God want to bless everyone, especially those who were pursuing Him? Why did He continue to allow upsetting things to happen?

I'm not sure I was ever able to sort this out. I know wonderful people who have had terrible trials in their life and mean people who continue to be blessed. But when I studied the Bible, there were countless stories about the hard times His great followers endured. The only way I could reconcile this was to acknowledge that God is sovereign and we don't get to know "why" many things happen. The one thing I did know was going through trials with God was much easier than going through them without Him.

12

SILVER LININGS

Now that I was married again and had to prepare for another trial, I needed to find a new attorney. My original attorney recommended a few and I eventually selected one. My first meeting with the new attorney was not good. He'd just stare at me as I was sharing details about Bill's crimes. I felt like he didn't believe me. I didn't like trying to convince someone, once again, that I was telling the truth.

I left the meeting feeling down, but the attorney called the next day and apologized for not believing me. He said he had checked some sources to make sure I wasn't lying because the story sounded pretty crazy. I decided to stay with him. First priority was to get as many concrete records of Bill's financial misconduct as I could to prepare for the upcoming trial.

During this time, Cory graduated from the University of Georgia. His hard work had paid off; he was graduating first in his class. I'll never know how he managed to do this with all the chaos and trips to see his father in prison, but I was so proud of him. Kinsey and I, my parents, my in laws, and my sister and her husband all went to his graduation. It was a time of welcome celebration.

Cory graduated in December and had an eight-month break before he planned to go to law school. He had been offered an internship in Germany to work on a marketing campaign for a brewery. He was excited; it would be a great and fun experience for a young man. I found myself having to make a very difficult decision.

I knew I really needed Cory's help because it would take a lot of time to find and organize all the documents for the upcoming trail. I also didn't want to deny him this opportunity in Germany. Kinsey was doing better but she was not available; she had transferred to Ohio State University and to my relief was doing well in her classes in interior design. I asked God, "What should I do?"

I had always encouraged the kids to embrace new opportunities and I never wanted to hold them back. I also sensed that Cory had a hard time talking about all that was going on, only because he felt so badly about it. I believed he imagined my life to be much worse than it really was and if he were home then he would be forced to see my life on a daily basis.

Yes, there were ongoing trials but great blessings, too. After much thought and prayer, I wrote Cory a note saying I needed him; this was new for me to ask for help and not at all easy. I added,

"I will understand if you decide to go to Germany and will never bring it up again."

Cory wrote back immediately to tell me he was coming home. I felt like I had just given the biggest gift in the world! He came home and got a job in the public defender's office in town, but spent most of his time trying to reconstruct his dad's criminal activity. He also studied for the LSAT (law school entrance exam). All his studying paid off; Cory was accepted at Duke University Law School. I was so proud!

Since I had no money to pay for school, Cory worked diligently to apply for every available scholarship and received enough money to pay for his tuition plus room and board. Cory spent that time before law school going through all his dad's office records. It was not a pretty picture. He also pulled up court documents and found out about other trials and property liens we had known nothing about.

It took seven months to get a solid financial picture of Bill's life. Cory documented that though large amounts of money funneled through the agency, the tax returns showed very little income. We were never able to figure out what else Bill was into. I even called his former administrative assistant to ask her what Bill really did.

She told me he was rarely in the office and spent a lot of time with several men who had prison records. I had a strong desire find out what Bill really did. After months of getting nowhere, a good friend asked me why I really wanted to know.

After thinking about this, I decided she was right. It was time to let go of the past and move on with my life.

Moving on took some effort and I wanted to reflect on all the good experiences I had enjoyed in the middle of the trials. This was healing and gave some much needed balance to my life. Many of these positive experiences took place during my visits to the kids in college. There was never an expectation I could get a hotel room, so I always stayed with them.

I have fond memories of sleeping with Kinsey in

her little single bed in the dorm. We would giggle and laugh and had so much fun. We both felt safe and so close as we snuggled in bed together. And, after all the giggling, when she finally fell asleep or before she woke up in the morning, I prayed from the depths of my heart as I said,

"Thank you, thank you, thank you God for protecting her!"

I always wanted to have a bigger word to let God know how much this meant to me; Kinsey was healing and I knew she would make it. Hours of prayers were said for Kinsey as she slept peacefully next to me. I also thanked God that she had decided to cut off communication with Bill. Although I wanted to respect how Cory and Kinsey handled their relationship with their dad, I knew Bill's dependence on her had been dragging her down.

One year when Kinsey was home from college, we decided to have a really fun summer. Each day we thought of something to do that was fun and free. We would do anything from having a picnic complete with candelabra, flowers and linen napkins, to shopping at the most expensive stores we could find knowing that we could not buy anything, to wading through a muddy creek.

We had a blast coming up with and doing these activities. We also came to enjoy what we called our freedom walks. On the days we learned something new and upsetting about Bill, we'd be either furious or despondent. Instead of allowing Bill to control us by giving him our emotions, we would go out walking at night.

First, we'd get everything off our chest that was bothering us and then we'd walk until we could both genuinely laugh. Sometimes these freedom walks were 30 minutes and sometimes they would go for two or more hours until we could laugh. This taught us how to not let someone else control our thinking.

Kinsey was always thinking of something fun and creative to delight me. Before she would go back to college she would hide encouraging notes all over the house. I always seemed to find them just when I needed them the most. One of my favorites will always be in a special location,

"She never once gave up. My mom is my hero."

She had no idea how much these notes meant to me! Kinsey was in interior design and would suggest, often late at night, that we redecorate a room in my house.

Of course money was very limited, but she would ask me lots of questions about what I liked and the next day while I was at work, she would paint, rearrange and transform rooms. What a delight to come home to find a beautiful new room! When I told her I wore the same clothes over and over again, she went in my closets, bought a few scarves and belts and put together my old clothes in creative ways so I felt like I gained a new wardrobe. All of this made me feel so special.

Kinsey also got a special surprise when she learned she could get college credit through Ohio State to spend a semester at sea. She asked me about going on this adventure and I said, "Yes," right away. What an unexpected blessing for her to travel on a freighter around the world and see and experience many countries while we were broke. God does have a good sense of humor!

I had just as many great times with Cory. As with Kinsey, he knew there was no money for me to stay in hotels during my visits. It is true that staying with a bunch of college guys was quite different from staying with Kinsey and her roommates, but equally fun. When I visited Cory at one of his apartments at the University of Georgia I noticed there were large frying pans on every table. I asked him about them.

Cory explained that they lived over the school garbage dump and there were many mice running around. They'd use the pans to whack the mice as they ran across the floor! I always appreciated that

Cory demanded that I be treated with respect. All the guys were to be fully dressed around me and not to use bad language.

Once when I was sleeping during a big party some drunken fraternity guy crawled in bed with me; obviously he wasn't expecting Cory's mom. I thought the other guys were going to kill him when they realized what had happened. The truth was I was much more afraid of a mouse than a drunken college guy. I realize this may not sound like much fun to others, but I have such good memories of these times.

I was concerned about some of the places Cory lived when he was in law school. During his first year he lived in a very shady apartment building. I helped him move in and thought it was so nice how the people sitting around on the steps helped us carry his furniture into the apartment. Little did I know they were only casing his place and belongings which were later trashed. In spite of this frugal living and hard studying, Cory had lots of friends, never lost his sense of humor and always knew how to have a fun time. I knew that his friends were genuine because he had nothing materially to offer.

Cory made sure each of my visits to see him was special. I knew taking me out to dinner was a big expense for him, but he always managed to find the money to do this or to plan a special event for me. He would get up early and go to the store to buy bagels, juice and fruit and then take me to a beautiful spot on campus where we would enjoy a picnic breakfast. He always had a good idea for something fun for us to do.

Cory also had an uncanny knack of making it seem like I was doing him a favor to accept the gifts he bought for me, with his hard-earned money. He had a new TV delivered to my house, saying he had to have it for a special ESPN game and hoped I didn't mind. He bought a new printer because he needed it for his legal briefs. He bought a new lawnmower because he was having allergy problems and wanted the yard cut shorter.

One of his better ones was when he bought me a new refrigerator. He told me his friends were embarrassed about my refrigerator, which I had repainted two times, and he didn't feel comfortable bringing more friends over until it was replaced. Of course, Cory had been living away and hadn't had friends over to the house for years, but I went along with his thoughtful game. Each of these gifts was a sacrifice for him and his kindness touched me more than he will ever know.

Now that I was living in my parents' house, the

summers were interesting. The home had just two bedrooms, and they took one while Cory, Kinsey and I shared the other. Kinsey and I shared the bed and Cory, when he was home, slept on a mattress on the floor. This wouldn't have been too bad except they had all their college belongings with them.

Needless to say it was very cozy with three of us plus everything they owned in one room. Believe me, there was not one inch of open floor space. I don't remember many arguments, but lots of laughter during that time; I felt like I got to have a sleepover every night with my two favorite people. My mom and dad could not have been better; either they were amazing actors or genuinely enjoyed having us live with them. We all have special memories of those summers!

13

FLYING PUZZLE PIECES

I had learned to accept life with its peaks and valleys. I enjoyed the peaks and leaned on God in the valleys. One unexpected valley happened late one night as Cory and I were getting ready to go to bed. There was a sudden and urgent pounding on the front door; when I opened it, I saw my neighbor's son, who was really upset. He asked if he could come in and I said, "Of course." I called for Cory to come downstairs; neither of us was prepared for what followed.

My neighbor, through his tears, said, "Your husband is in love with my mom and he has been calling her every day from prison."

He added, "They will probably be getting married once he gets out."

I was in disbelief. His mom and I were friends; she had asked me over for dinner many evenings while Bill was in prison; she knew the real story. As if this wasn't a big enough shock, the bigger shock was if they did get married they would be living across the street from me.

I did the best I could to comfort my neighbor's son, who was angry, while dealing with my own feelings. After he left, Cory and I sat in silence because neither one of us knew what to say. I was numb as I got ready for bed and pleaded with God,

"Certainly, You would never let this happen!"

A few months later I received a notice saying that Bill would be moving into a halfway house in Toledo. Cory and I were still in the midst of preparing for the trial and this added more stress to the situation. Bill did move into the halfway house and three months later was officially released from the prison system. He bought a little house nearby, I'm not sure with what, but most of the time he was across the street with my friend. This was a very low time for me. I would look out the window and see the two of them dressed up to go to an event, having a family BBQ, or talking with the neighbors.

The intensity of my emotions at this time scared me. God and I did much wrestling. My previous prayers turned into raw conversations where I unloaded on Him,

"God, what in the world are you thinking. For the past two years I have been in survival mode, endured countless depositions, defended myself over and over again in court trials all due to Bill's criminal activity. I've lost my home and everything I owned, worked any extra jobs I could find to barely scrape by and did everything I knew to do to keep the family together. I worried myself sick about Cory and Kinsey. And, now You let Bill waltz out of prison and I have to watch him daily right across the street enjoying his life with my girlfriend!"

I went on, "Is this some kind of a test? I'm getting sick and tired of all these tests and this current situation is just plain cruel. Are you waiting to see how much it takes to make me crack?"

Mad was much too mild to describe how I felt at this time. To make it worse, I felt stalked, as Bill was constantly looking out of the window at me when I was outside, or going to, or coming home from work, or other activities. He would leave upsetting notes or phone messages about a variety of things such as, "Who were those weird friends you had over last night? Can't you do better than that?"

Or, "Your hair looks terrible, you need to go to someone and do something about it."

Or, the worst ones were, "You have ruined my life and stolen my kids from me."

My life was shattered and I felt threatened as Bill's accusations continued. Bill had also put together a long list of everything, in his opinion, that I had done wrong in our marriage and mailed it to every friend we ever had, as well as to some people at work. The letter was filled with lies but things were explained in such detail they sounded believable. I was angry and humiliated.

I asked many times, "Where are you, God?"

Additionally, I was having challenges at work. I had taken on the leadership of our diversity initiative. This was uncharted territory for me and I didn't know how to handle the fall-out that came as a result of this initiative. So, work was taxing and then I'd come home to more stress. I was very anxious. I said,

"God, when is enough, enough?"

I wish I could tell you God answered these questions and things quickly turned around. They didn't. I learned another hard lesson: I need to trust God even when I hate what is going on. I needed a lot of grace for this one!

Finally the trial to prove Bill's financial misconduct came up; Bill had delayed it as many times as he could but we had a final, firm date. Kinsey came up from Ohio State and Cory drove up from Duke University in Durham, North Carolina. My sister and her husband also came up to be with me. This support was so appreciated!

As soon as I arrived at the courthouse, my attorney asked me to settle, which basically meant giving money to Bill, to avoid going to trial. I had been asked to do this before and was tired of it. A rational response to my attorney's request would have been to say yes, because the trail was scheduled to go for five days and was going to cost way more than any settlement. But something in me snapped and I said,

"No, I've had it, no more settling, we are going to trial."

My attorney looked at me and said, "You are a very foolish woman. A five-day trial is going to cost you thousands of dollars, which you don't have."

Frankly, at that point I could have cared less about what my attorney or Bill wanted. The trial was to start that afternoon. As it turned out, Bill was so emotionally upset his attorney said he was in no state to withstand a trial; he asked for yet another extension.

It was very easy for me to say, "No!"

This didn't stem from a lack of forgiveness but from a desire to be finished. I wanted the truth to come out, once and for all. The trial began that afternoon but had to be cut short, I was told, due to Bill's emotional state. Turned out, I didn't have to pay him anything. I should have felt relief, but I only experienced disappointment. After months of preparation this was an opportunity to find out the truth about many things. Now I would never know.

My family stayed by my side the whole time. They ate dinner with me that night and then by 9 p.m. everyone was gone. I was restless and felt very alone. Around 2 a.m. I decided to take a long walk because I had a lot of things to discuss with God. When I was about a mile from home, I silently yelled,

"Okay, so what was that all about? My life has been turned inside out for the past six years. I've lost my marriage and everything I own, and my kids and family have been deeply hurt. After seven months of preparing for this trial it would have been nice to get some answers, and I didn't even get that. This is total crap and I don't understand what You are thinking."

I realize this sounds pretty raw and disrespectful, but I figured He already knew what I was thinking, plus we had had many heart-to-hearts. God had never turned His back on me and I was confident He wouldn't leave me now. It's hard to explain exactly what happened next, but a flood of messages came rushing into me. It felt like I had an hour of messages compressed into a few minutes. It was so profound I came home and wrote down everything. God told me four things:

o "First, I took things out of you that you asked Me to." He said "You were struggling to forgive Bill and you were also dealing with jealousy when all your friends were doing fun things and you weren't able join them. I answered your prayers and took these roots out of you."

o "Second, I took things out of you that you didn't know you had in you." God reminded me, "You had lots of issues around pride. These were invisible to you to the point that you were even proud of your pride, which you saw as great resourcefulness. I showed you this and am helping you deal with it."

o "Third, I am putting things in you that you think you already have." God said, "You thought you were good at love, but it's nothing compared to My love. I am teaching you to love the way I do."

o "Fourth, I am putting things in you that you have asked Me to." God reminded me, "You have asked Me to give you wisdom and I am doing this."

That split second when God pushed all those messages into my heart and head was incredible. I've never experienced anything like it before or since. In a flash I felt like pieces from a puzzle were flying together at a high rate of speed into one design. God had brought up many specific examples, which were the individual puzzle pieces, ones that He allowed and used to transform me.

Suddenly, many things that had previously confused me and made me angry, now made sense. I had a fresh revelation of how God had been working on me for the past seven years to change my thinking and my heart. I knew these changes would have never happened without major trials.

I understood at a deeper level how much God loved me and was cheering me on every day, even if I didn't always see it. I was humbled. I felt grateful and intensely loved. In a flash my anger and confusion were replaced with a deep sense of peace. I finished my walk and went home. That night I slept soundly until late the next day. When I woke up I had a new and positive anticipation about my future and I was ready to embrace it!

LYNN'S STORY

14

GOD'S TAPESTRY

Though life still had its ups and downs, as I embraced my future I had more strength and peace during the low times. My journey continued to unfold, but instead of "flying puzzle pieces," I began to see the weaving of a tapestry, which early on can be messy and ugly with all the bumps, knots and different threads, including the ones that had to be cut off and discarded.

At some point, I saw the jumbled frayed threads were making a beautiful design, one I could have never imagined. This describes my journey: after years of mess, I slowly started to see and understand a tapestry was being made, and my struggles were necessary to make a rich design. This insight gave me the courage to keep moving forward.

I now believe God has a signature "tapestry" for each one of us. He knows exactly where He wants us to go, but must orchestrate many circumstances in our lives in order for us to get there. His patience and love are amazing. He gives us many opportunities to pass each test, unlike school, where one failed test can permanently affect your record.

One test I couldn't seem to pass was not to care what people said and thought about me. God knew I would need many opportunities to pass this. One day when I was really upset about something that happened at work, I slipped out of the office and went to the gym where I just started walking around the track in my work clothes. I'm sure I looked ridiculous but I didn't care.

As I was circling the track over and over again I heard, "How long are you going to keep going around this same mountain?"

I asked, "What mountain?"

God gently replied, "The mountain is how much value you put on what people say about you. You need to listen to who I say you are and not who others say you are."

That day I got a revelation God had been putting me

in situations where some people were not pleased with what I was doing because He wanted me to get over being a people pleaser. It took me a while, but I finally saw it. He knew exactly what was needed to help me break free from this. Although I can still struggle with this issue, I know my identity is in Him and not in what others think about me.

God has restored and transformed me during the years of struggle. It makes me think of those gold strands in the tapestry that look most beautiful when they are contrasted against the dark threads which, for me, represent my trials.

I remember telling Cory and Kinsey, "I would never trade my life right now for my 'perfect' past life. God has taught me so much and I would never go back."

God has restored many things since that final court trial. Here are just a few examples:

o Bill stayed in the neighborhood about one year and then met another woman, got married and moved out of state. God had removed my inability to forgive Bill, something I was unable to do for myself. Although I chose to have no contact with Bill, I released him in my heart, and thus freed myself. It was only through God's grace that I could forgive Bill.

o Cory graduated with a Law and MBA
degree from Duke University. He married a
wonderful woman and they live in New
York City. They recently had their first child
and I have the honor of being a
grandmother.

Kinsey graduated in interior design from
Ohio State University and has been blessed
with many creative, fun and interesting jobs
in her field. She is married and currently
living in Las Vegas. I am so touched by all
the love and support my children have given
me over the years.

As stated earlier, I knew crises would either
tear our family apart or strengthen it. The
bond between us is so strong and my
children continue to give me much joy. If
it's true, which I know it is, that God's love
is far greater than ours, I can't begin to
imagine what this must be like as I have
trouble finding words big enough to express
how much I love my children.

o I received a promotion at work that I never
knew was coming. I was promoted to
manage the training function. I believe if
someone had asked me if I wanted this
position I would have said, "No," because so
much was still going on and I didn't want to
be an example of the Peter Principle, where

people are promoted to their level of incompetence.

It has been a blessing to work almost 30 years for this great company. This (public) company's Mission Statement says, "We serve God by serving others." This was important to me when I joined the company but continued to mean more as time went on.

It's interesting how God can give us things we never even ask for. I had never thought about having a real career; my interest was to find something challenging to do and make money doing it. He gave me a wonderful career at a company with strong values, and I am very grateful.

o Since I was living in my parents' house, I had many opportunities to see my mom and dad, especially during summers when they were home from Florida. It's interesting how little we know about our own parents.

This close contact forged an even deeper and richer relationship than we already had. I got to be there when my dad died in the comfort and security of his own home, with his family by his side. After my dad passed away, my mom wanted to move into an "independent living" home to be with other seniors.

One Sunday, God put it in my heart to call her and ask her if we could have a "date night" every week. I was busy but getting better at listening to Him so I got my call in just before she went to bed. As expected, she was delighted about our upcoming date nights.

The next morning, the staff where she lived called to tell me my mom had been rushed to the hospital because they thought she was having a heart attack. Fortunately, things weren't as serious as originally thought and she was home in a few days. I realized how differently my call for weekly dates would have been perceived coming after this scare versus before. My mom and I had "date nights" every Wednesday for six years and I will always treasure that special time with her.

o Of my many good work experiences, two stand out. The best one was when I got to work with a team to figure out how to train employees on the company's values. This meant a lot to me because I believe people are desperately looking for companies that manifest values. This was a career highlight and I felt honored to co-facilitate this values course with our executives.

o The second experience was a growth one where I was working on the diversity/inclusion effort at the company. During this time, my learning curve was very high as I learned much about myself, both good and bad, and had to maneuver through the landmines that this sensitive topic can expose.

In some respects it mimicked the moment I realized how much pride I had. I had always considered myself knowledgeable in diversity issues and it took some shaking to realize that I knew much less than I thought. Once I was able to humble myself, I started enjoying a new learning journey. God provided some great mentors to coach me during that time.

o My mom died eight years after my father. My parents gave me their house after their deaths; of course they did something equally nice for my brother and sister. Wow, what a blessing, it hadn't been that long ago when I had had no idea where I was going to live and now I had this amazing home!

When I had been at my lowest points, I would make lists of what I would want in a home if I were ever able to afford one. It consisted of things like a small private back yard, a neighborhood that was pretty and safe for walking, a special window seat for reading, a connected garage, lots of light, etc. My parents' house had everything on this list and even more. I never dreamed this would happen and am thankful every day.

o I have been financially restored. I now have a house, a good job, and all debts have been paid off. I am back on my feet and am able to "pay it forward" by giving gifts to others, mostly anonymous ones, and though it's still hard, I continue to get better at accepting help.

o I've always had a sense of adventure and love to travel where I can see different places and experience new cultures. I was certain that my travel days were over, but God has opened many doors to bless me.

Some of the places I have been able to go include: Greece, France, Thailand, Italy, Switzerland, Netherlands, India, Belgium and Israel. One of my very best surprises was when Cory and Kinsey rented a cottage on a lake for my 60th birthday. They asked family members to come up whenever they could during the week and it was an amazing time. Once again, my children continue to delight me in ways I never expect.

o Although I occasionally go to counseling, I am healed, experience joy and can once again help others. This is a great honor and I don't take it lightly. God has given me a much deeper understanding about issues that people go through and I have a greater compassion and desire to be of help. I am humbled and grateful for the support I have received and now make it a priority to support others.

I've shared many outward ways that God has restored me, but the greatest restoration by far has been a changed heart. Through the trials, I learned about the "fruits of the spirit:" love, joy, peace, longsuffering, kindness, goodness, faithfulness, gentleness and self control.

I've heard it said God helps us with the first three, but it is through longsuffering that the next five are developed. This takes time and is a journey. I learned how different God's timetable was from mine; He is taking much more time to develop my character than I would have imagined.

I've also been much more in touch with God's grace, love and desire to have a relationship with me during these years. It's pretty overwhelming to think the One who created the universe really wants to spend time with me/us.

Just as we want to be involved with our children's

lives, He wants to be involved in ours. God has taught me to know, love and trust Him and this took time. I've often wondered, "Can you really get to know and trust God if you think you don't need Him?" I don't believe you can. I'm okay with the fact that I was a "foxhole Christian" and that it was only through tough times that I drew close to Him.

Even though my life has changed dramatically, I wouldn't trade it. God has switched up "my" plans. We are on a new journey and I am not even sure where we're going. I've given Him control and I don't know what He has in store for me. It used to be unsettling to not have things planned out and be in control, at least in my own mind. This makes me think of that original question I asked my pastor so many years ago:

"What is faith?"

I now know faith is trusting that God always has my best interests in mind, even when I don't know, understand or like what is going on. Although I had "head knowledge" of this concept, it has taken years for it to drop those 12 inches to my heart, and on any given day, I still experience doubt. I'm finding life with God is both interesting and exciting.

This poem does a great job of describing my journey.

A Tandem Ride With God (author unknown)

I used to think of God as my observer, my judge, keeping track of the things I did wrong, so as to know whether I merited heaven or hell when I die.

He was out there, sort of like a president. I recognized His picture when I saw it, but I didn't really know Him.

But later on, when I met Jesus, it seemed as though life was rather like a bike, but it was a tandem bike, and I noticed Jesus was in the back helping me pedal.

I didn't know just when it was He suggested we change, but life has not been the same since I took the back-seat to Jesus, my Lord. He makes life exciting.

When I had control, I thought I knew the way. It was rather boring, but predictable. It was the shortest distance between two points.

But when He took the lead, He knew delightful long cuts, up mountains, and through rocky places and at break-through speeds; it was all I could do to hang on!

Even though it often looked like madness, He said, "Pedal!" I was worried and anxious and asked, "Where are you taking me?" He laughed and didn't answer and I started to learn to trust.

I forgot my boring life and entered into adventure. And when I'd say, "I'm scared," He'd lean back and touch my hand.

He took me to people with gifts that I needed, gifts of healing, acceptance and joy. They gave me their gifts to take on my journey, our journey, my Lord's and mine.

And we were off again. He said, "Give the gifts away; they're extra baggage, too much weight." So I did, to the people we met, and I found in giving I received, and still our burden was light.

I did not trust Him, at first, in control of my life. I thought He'd wreck it, but He knows bike secrets, knows how to make it bend to take sharp corners, jump to clear high rocks, fly to shorten scary passages.

And I am learning to shut up and pedal in the strangest places, and I'm beginning to enjoy the view and the cool breeze on my face with my delightful constant companion, Jesus.

And when I'm sure I just can't do any more, He just smiles and says... "Pedal"

(Author unknown)

15

JUST ASK

This story chronicles my journey of coming into relationship with God. Yours will be perfectly planned for you. Making a tapestry is a process; one that has taken much longer that I thought it would, and will continue for my lifetime. But I wouldn't trade any of it. Always know that you are never alone, even though it may feel like it at times. Reach out to God and to others when life takes a difficult and unexpected turn. He wants to guide and help you, comfort you, and most of all to love you. All you have to do is ask Him - and then get ready for quite a ride!

ABOUT THE AUTHOR

Lynn Kampfer, 64, is a survivor. She loves to travel, swim and visit with friends. She married right after graduating from The Ohio State University, and then received a Master of Education degree from The University of Toledo. For nearly 30 years, Lynn worked as the Manager of Learning and Development for a large agribusiness. She retired in February 2014. Lynn is involved in her church and various community activities. Her two grown children are the loves of her life.

Made in the USA
Lexington, KY
18 September 2017